W9-BSH-104

Supreme Court Confirmation Hearings in the U.S. Senate

The idea that Supreme Court nominees might not be forthcoming during their testimony before the Senate Judiciary Committee has profound implications for American democracy. Yet critics claim that nominees have become more evasive in recent decades, and Senate confirmation hearings are routinely derided as "exercises in obfuscation," devoid of real substance. But do today's nominees really sidestep more questions than their predecessors?

Conducting a line-by-line analysis of every confirmation hearing since 1955—an original dataset of nearly 11,000 questions and answers—Dion Farganis and Justin Wedeking discover that nominees are far more forthcoming than generally assumed. Applying a scoring system they developed to assess each nominee's testimony based on the same criteria, they find that some of the earliest nominees were actually *less* willing to answer questions than their contemporary counterparts. Further, they argue that a number of factors—including changes in the political culture of Congress and the 1981 introduction of televised coverage of the hearings—have created the impression that nominee candor is in decline. Lastly, they show that despite what senators often claim, their votes are driven more by party and ideology than by a nominee's responsiveness to their questions. Changes in the confirmation process intersect with increasing levels of party polarization as well as constituents' more informed awareness and opinions of recent Supreme Court nominees.

Dion Farganis is Assistant Professor of Political Science at Elon University.

Justin Wedeking is Associate Professor of Political Science at the University of Kentucky.

Supreme Court Confirmation Hearings in the U.S. Senate

RECONSIDERING THE CHARADE

Dion Farganis and Justin Wedeking

THE UNIVERSITY OF MICHIGAN PRESS

ANN ARBOR

Copyright © by the University of Michigan 2014
All rights reserved

This book may not be reproduced, in whole or in part, including illustrations, in any form
(beyond that copying permitted by Sections 107 and 108 of the U.S. Copyright Law and
except by reviewers for the public press), without written permission from the publisher.

Published in the United States of America by
The University of Michigan Press
Manufactured in the United States of America
⊗ Printed on acid-free paper

2017   2016   2015   2014   4   3   2   1

A CIP catalog record for this book is available from the British Library.

Library of Congress Cataloging-in-Publication Data

Farganis, Dion, author.
  Supreme Court confirmation hearings in the U.S. Senate : reconsidering the charade /
Dion Farganis and Justin Wedeking.
    pages   cm.
  Includes bibliographical references and index.
  ISBN 978-0-472-11933-2 (hardcover : alk. paper) — ISBN 978-0-472-12027-7 (e-book)
    1. United States. Supreme Court—Officials and employees—Selection and appoint-
ment.   2. Judges—Selection and appointment—United States.   3. United States. Con-
gress. Senate. Committee on the Judiciary.   4. Legislative hearings—United States.
I. Wedeking, Justin, author.   II. Title.
KF8742.F37   2014
328.7307'45—dc23

                                                    2013048569

For, and because of, my family. —Dion

For Maya and my brother Josh. —Justin

Contents

Acknowledgments

Although we attended the same graduate school, shared an office, occasionally discussed sports, and both left Minnesota in 2007, this project did not begin until several years later when we were many miles apart and had not spoken in some time. Thanks to the miracle of the Internet, however, what started as a loosely formed idea about the "Ginsburg Rule" quickly turned into a fairly coherent research plan—and by the time that Elena Kagan was testifying, we were fielding calls from national media organizations. And now, after many years, three kids (one for Farganis, and two additions for Wedeking), countless disagreements about whose football team truly reigns supreme, and more e-mails than either of us care to admit, we have finally achieved our goal with the publication of this book.

This book would not have been possible without the help of many good people. First, we thank Melody Herr and the wonderful staff at the University of Michigan Press. Melody's guidance as an editor from start to finish was impeccable, and we would not have made it to the finish line without her calming reassurance and patience.

For their comments or substantive advice on the manuscript, which greatly improved our thinking on it (and we hope the final product as well), we thank Ryan Black, Paul Collins, Mike Fix, Linda Greenhouse, Jason Husser, Timothy Johnson, Jonathan Kastellec, Orin Kerr, Wendy Martinek, Garrison Nelson, Ryan Owens, Jeff Peake, Lori Ringhand, Jason Roberts, Elliot Slotnick, Geoffrey Stone, Clayton Thyne, Art Ward, the anonymous reviewers of the manuscript, and many others who were patient enough to provide us with comments and encouragement. We also thank Jasmine Farrier, Daniel Lempert, Steve Wasby, and Steve Wermiel for answering our question on information regarding William Brennan's Judiciary Committee vote. Of course, none of these people are responsible for the interpretations or results in this book. Any and all errors are very much our own doing.

For research assistance we thank Mark Ingles for help in coding a portion of the nominee exchanges. We also thank Cody Hollan for his work gathering *New York Times* data.

Although we collected a large amount of data for this book, we also acknowledge that by itself, it would not be nearly as insightful or helpful unless we could use it in combination with several previous sources. Specifically, we thank Lee Epstein and Jeff Segal for answering questions about interest group data and data on the nominees, and for making their data readily available.

We also acknowledge our earlier publications on this topic. Even though this book is considerably different than our previous work, an early version of some of our arguments in this book were published as "'No Hints, No Forecasts, No Previews': An Empirical Analysis of Supreme Court Nominee Candor from Harlan to Kagan," *Law and Society Review* 45, no. 3 (2011): 525–60; and "The Candor Factor: Does Nominee Evasiveness Affect Judiciary Committee Support for Supreme Court Nominees?" *Hofstra Law Review* 39, no 2 (2010): 329–68. We also presented early versions of our work at the 2010 American Political Science Association annual meeting in Washington, D.C., and the 2010 Midwest Political Science Association annual meeting in Chicago.

On a more personal level, Farganis wishes to thank his departmental colleagues for their insights and ideas, and Elon University for its generous research funding. He also wishes to thank his parents, who taught him how to think, and his sister for being such a pillar of support. As with any Farganis project, a special word must go out to Gordon Silverstein, mentor and friend, who rarely takes credit but deserves much of it. And lastly, a note of unparalleled gratitude to Rachel Farganis, who has for nearly five years put up with boxes of marked-up confirmation hearing transcripts cluttering the house, and, more important, has been there every day as a partner, sounding board, and source of inspiration. When this project began, Rachel and I were not yet married; now we have a son. I hope that someday Niko reads this book and knows that it would not have been possible were it not for the sacrifices that his mother made along the way.

Wedeking thanks his colleagues for providing support and the Department of Political Science and the University of Kentucky for providing time and resources to work on this manuscript. He would also like to acknowledge a 2011 Summer Faculty Research Fellowship from the College of Arts and Sciences that provided summer salary that enabled him to focus considerable time on the project. He also thanks his wife, Michelle, for her continued support and putting up with a long string of "just let me finish one more thing[s]" that has gone on for several years now. Without her support, Wedeking's progress would be clicking along at a glacial pace. Wedeking also thanks his three daughters—Megan, Lauren, and Maya—for bringing joy to his life. And more importantly, for continually reminding him of what is important in life. Finally, he dedicates this book to his newest daughter, Maya, and to his big brother Josh for being everything a little brother could ask for.

ONE

A Vapid and Hollow Charade?

One can only speculate about Elena Kagan's first thoughts when she learned in May 2010 that she would be nominated to replace the retiring John Paul Stevens on the U.S. Supreme Court, and thus soon face a Senate confirmation process. But it seems safe to assume that it did not take long for the words "vapid and hollow charade" to come to mind.

More than a decade earlier, that was how Kagan had described modern Supreme Court confirmation hearings in a widely read law review article. Earlier hearings were "serious discussion[s]," Kagan claimed, but since the 1980s the proceedings had been dominated by nominees who provided only "evasive answers," "platitudes," and "personal anecdotes" (Kagan 1995, 941). As a result, the confirmation process had completely lost its "educative function" with respect to the public. Instead of helping Americans make informed assessments of their Supreme Court nominees, the hearings now merely reinforced "lessons of cynicism" that all too often plague American political life (941). Simply put, until nominees were once again willing to answer tough questions, the hearings would have little or no value.

Whether Kagan would apply this high standard to her own testimony was one of the most anticipated storylines of her confirmation hearing. Ultimately, it turned out to be much less of an issue than expected, in large part because Kagan walked back somewhat from her earlier views, telling the Judiciary Committee that she never meant to suggest that prospective justices should have to discuss their views on pending cases (Kagan 2010, 6).

But the larger point—the one that provides not only the title but the motivation for this book—is that Kagan's characterization of the post-1980s hearings as a "vapid and hollow charade" enjoys nearly universal assent among scholars, pundits, senators, and just about anyone else who follows the Supreme Court confirmation process. The precise descriptions themselves may vary—from "exercise[s] in obfuscation" (Yalof 2008) to a "'kabuki' dance" (Fitzpatrick 2009), a "farce" (Benson 2010), or simply a "mess" (Carter 1988)—but the basic idea is the same: Supreme Court nominees are no longer forthcoming during their testimony, and Supreme Court confirmation hearings are no longer working properly as a result.

For all of its popularity, however, this rather grim assessment of the hearings has at least one rather glaring problem: it is not all that accurate. What Kagan and so many other critics *assume* is that nominees today answer fewer questions—that they are more "evasive," in Kagan's own words—than their predecessors. Indeed, the entire chorus of criticism surrounding the confirmation hearing process is predicated on the belief that there was a time when the hearings were more substantive, but that in the 1980s nominees began strategically avoiding controversial queries that could sink their confirmation prospects.

But as we reveal in this book, that is not really what happened. As it turns out, Supreme Court nominees have actually been answering questions in roughly the same way since the hearings began in the mid-1950s, more than a half century ago. Moreover, nominees are not nearly as evasive as we have been led to believe. On average, they only refuse to respond to about one out of every ten questions they are asked, and they give forthcoming answers to nearly seven out of those ten. Thus while they may not be perfectly candid all of the time, Supreme Court nominees are much more responsive during their hearings than previously assumed. The conventional wisdom needs to be rethought.

To be fair to Kagan and all of those who share her view, this hearings-in-decline narrative certainly seems logical enough. Even casual Court watchers remember Robert Bork's long and candid testimony in 1987, which revealed a conservative judicial philosophy too far outside the mainstream for senators to support. In the wake of this, it would only be natural for subsequent nominees to be reticent and cagey in their responses. "Say too much and get rejected" seemed to be the lesson of the Bork hearings.

But Bork's confirmation hearing was not the turning point that most people assume it to be. Nominees long before the 1980s were exhibiting comparable degrees of candor, and nominees since Bork have *not* been dramatically less forthcoming. Bork was an outlier, but not one with nearly the effect that the conventional wisdom suggests. Nominee testimony—how forthcoming nominees are when they answer Judiciary Committee questions—looks largely the same both before and after the 1980s.

None of this is to suggest that the hearings have not changed over time. They have. They are much longer than they used to be: more senators ask more questions today than in years past. And they are more structured: each member of the Judiciary Committee now asks questions, in order—a far cry from the relative free-for-all that characterized earlier proceedings—and the voting tends to fall along party lines more than it used to. The questions have changed as well, reflecting the types of issues that are important to Americans at any given time (Ringhand and Collins 2011).

All of these structural shifts can be traced to the introduction of television cameras into the hearing room in 1981, however, and not to any dramatic changes in the ways that nominees have approached their testimony. Thus on that key issue—the degree to which nominees answer questions—our research shows that surprisingly little has changed in the past 60 years.

Previous Work on the Confirmation Hearings

Although this book offers what we believe to be a significant step forward in understanding Supreme Court confirmation hearings, we are not the first to tackle the topic. The majority of this work has been prescriptive in nature, focusing on shortcomings in the confirmation process and recommending proposals for changing it. Some scholars working in this vein argue that in the interest of judicial independence, Supreme Court nominees should not be required to answer questions about how they would rule in specific cases. Most famously, perhaps, Stephen Carter (1988) urges a circumscribed role for Senate questioning, arguing that senators should confine themselves to learning about a nominee's basic qualifications and his or her "background moral vision and the capacity for moral reflection" (1199). Others envision a slightly more robust role for the Senate that includes inquiries into the nominee's judicial philosophy or general approach to constitutional interpretation (Eisgruber 2007; Goldberg 2004; Tribe 2005). A third group, spearheaded by Post and Siegel (2006), contends that senators should be allowed to ask nominees about how they would have voted in cases that have already been decided by the Supreme Court.

Much less empirical research has been done on the hearings themselves, however. A handful of these studies focus on the questions asked by the Judiciary Committee. Here the recent work of Ringhand and Collins (2011) stands out. Among their most illuminating findings, Ringhand and Collins report that women and minority nominees face very different kinds of questions from committee members. They also reveal that questions about racial discrimination have decreased over time, while questions about gender and sexual orientation have increased. By contrast, an earlier study by Guliuzza, Reagan, and Barrett (1994) found that questioning had not changed all that much—at least at a general level—over time. But Williams and Baum (2006) offer support for Ringhand and Collins's finding that nominees now face more questions about their past judicial decisions than in years past.

Unfortunately, research exploring how nominees *respond* to the Judiciary Committee's questions has been scarce. One study by Ringhand (2008) examines how the nine justices on the final Rehnquist Court, during their confirmation hearings, answered questions about past Supreme Court cases, and finds that while nominees often responded to these questions, they also frequently invoked their "privilege" not to answer. Along similar lines, Czarnezki, Ford, and Ringhand (2006), also look at the Rehnquist Court justices' confirmation hearings, and find that, by and large, nominee answers are not a reliable indicator of how the justice will vote on cases. But to the best of our knowledge, no previous work has examined all types of nominee responses, all of the hearings, or both.

Changing the Way We Look at Confirmation Hearings

In this book, we provide the first large-scale empirical analysis of nominee responsiveness, or "candor," from the time that regular Supreme Court confirmation hearings began in 1955 until today. By carefully coding every question and answer from every hearing from John Marshall Harlan II through Elena Kagan—nearly 11,000 observations in total—we were able to discover that Supreme Court nominees have not, in fact, become dramatically less forthcoming in recent years, and that the hearings are not nearly as "vapid and hollow" as the conventional wisdom suggests. In the chapters that follow, we explain exactly how we came to this somewhat surprising set of conclusions, why we think this is important, and how we think our findings change the debate about both the past and the future of Supreme Court confirmation hearings.

We begin in chapter 2 by tracing the development of the hearings from a historical perspective. Even the most seasoned court watchers are sometimes surprised to learn that public hearings for Supreme Court justices did not become a fixed part of the confirmation process until the mid-1950s.[1] A few nominees had hearings prior to this time, but after the Court's intensely controversial 1954 ruling in *Brown v. Board of Education*, every nominee has appeared and testified.[2] At first, the hearings attracted little attention from either the press or the public. But because of a number of key historical events—most notably, perhaps, the introduction of televised coverage in the 1980s—the hearings today are much more high profile, contentious, and longer affairs. We walk through several of these historical developments to show how each has helped make the hearings what they are today.

Of particular interest is the degree to which the Judiciary Committee's questioning has changed over the years. Early nominees, from the 1950s through the 1960s, were asked as few as six questions; a "long" hearing would be 100 questions and answers. Recent proceedings (from 2005 through 2010), by contrast, have ranged between 500 and 700 questions. Moreover, in earlier hearings, questioning was often dominated by a single senator or a handful of senators. But since the 1980s the questioning has been much more evenly distributed; committee members rarely if ever leave any of their allotted time unused. Again, most of these "structural" changes to the hearings occurred when televised coverage began in 1981. Our view is that this is not coincidental: senators ask more questions—and, depending on party considerations, more difficult questions—because they know that their constituents (and millions of other Americans) are watching. In short, television helps senators with their reelection goals (see, e.g., Mayhew 1974).

But if the questioning has evolved over time, what about the answers? As senators have become more exacting, have nominees become more evasive? In chapters 3 and 4, we focus on this crucial part of the story. We start in chapter 3 by explaining our method for examining and analyzing nominee testimony. The approach that we used was fairly straightforward: we coded each exchange between a senator and nominee, recording among other things the topic of the question, the degree to which the answer was forthcoming, and, if it was not forthcoming, what reason the nominee gave for not answering fully. All told, we analyzed nearly 11,000 exchanges, giving us the first complete database of Supreme Court confirmation hearing testimony—every question and answer coded for every hearing since 1955.

In chapter 4, we turn to our central inquiry: Have nominees become significantly less forthcoming over time, as the conventional wisdom suggests? The short answer, we discover, is no. Roughly speaking, responsiveness has been fairly stable over time, with most nominees answering more than 60 percent of questions without any qualification or hesitation at all. Outright nonresponsiveness, it turns out, is quite rare both for recent nominees and their predecessors. Nominees from Harlan to Kagan have, on balance, been better about answering questions than we expected. And while there has been a slight decline in responsiveness since the Bork hearings, it is nothing on the level of what we had been led to believe by critics.

That said, some nominees have been more forthcoming than others. Therefore, we look for answers to why this variation exists, and find one very compelling explanation: questions about civil liberties and civil rights issues (e.g., free speech, abortion, and affirmative action) tend to drive down nominee candor levels more than other questions. This, in turn, may help explain why there is such a strong *perception* that nominees have become less forthcoming of late: civil liberties and civil rights questions have increased gradually over the years, pushing nominee responsiveness down slightly. But since those types of questions tend to be the most carefully watched exchanges, there is a heightened sense that nominees are answering far fewer questions than they did in years past. Overall, however, our view is that the empirical record does not support the characterization of the hearings as "vapid and hollow." At the very least, we believe, if one considers today's hearings to be vapid and hollow, one would also have to say the same about earlier hearings as well.

Having dispelled the myth that recent Supreme Court nominees have become dramatically more evasive, we turn our attention in chapter 5 to the relationship between a nominee's testimony and the Judiciary Committee's vote. It is not uncommon today for senators to claim that their confirmation vote is based on the degree to which the nominee is forthcoming during his or her hearings. For example, as Senator Chuck Schumer told John Roberts in 2005, "[T]he first criterion upon which I will base my vote is whether you will answer questions fully and forthrightly" (Roberts 2005b, 39). But is this in fact the case? Here we make one of our most surprising discoveries: Since the early 1980s, voting has been driven much more by partisanship than by the nominee's actual responsiveness during the hearing. Nominee responsiveness was more of a factor in committee voting *prior* to the 1980s than it is today. In fact, in recent years, responsiveness is not statistically related to how senators vote. What is more surprising, perhaps, is that partisanship played little systematic role in voting prior to the 1980s (though ideology did). This finding calls into question one of the central narratives of the modern confirmation hearings—that nominee responsiveness matters. Instead, as the Senate has become more polarized, and as the hearings have become much more widely watched because of television, the role of ideology in committee voting has increased and the impact of nominee candor has decreased. Thus despite what many current Committee members may want the nominees to believe, the decision on how to vote is probably determined in advance, and is not the result of how forthcoming or evasive a nominee is during his or her testimony.

All of this leaves us with at least one important unanswered question. If nominees today are not significantly more evasive than in years past, then what exactly is driving the *perception*—a widespread one, to say the least—that the hearings have become so "vapid and hollow?" In chapter 6, we identify three factors that have led to this misperception. First and foremost, hearings before 1981 were not televised, and little attention was paid to them. As a result, critics have a tendency to romanticize earlier proceedings, significantly "rounding up" the degree to which nominees before the first televised hearings for Sandra Day O'Connor, answered questions—which has made recent hearings look less substantive by comparison. Second, when they do not answer questions, nominees have increasingly offered two excuses—the issue could come before the Court, or they do not know enough to answer—both of which critics apparently perceive to be particularly evasive. And lastly, the public appetite for answers from nominees is incredibly strong, as indicated by public opinion survey data. Together, these three factors have created a kind of "perfect storm" whereby recent nominee performances have been framed as being significantly less forthcoming and less substantive than earlier nominees, when in fact the differences are not that great.

In chapter 7, we explore some of the normative and practical implications of our findings. By design, the Senate's "advice and consent" role in judicial confirmations is supposed to provide an element of "democratic accountability" to the unelected Court by ensuring that the people have some voice, however indirect it might be, in who becomes a justice (Post and Siegel 2006, 39). But if the hearings are just a charade, and nominees are no longer answering questions, then that democratic accountability is lost. This is why, from a normative perspective at least, we think it is so important to determine whether prospective justices are indeed less forthcoming today. Functional and meaningful confirmation hearings serve an important purpose in American democracy, and a loss of public faith in the hearings carries serious consequences. As such, if the hearings are not in fact "broken," this is important for the public to know.

We then turn to the ways in which our findings might influence the ongoing debate about how the hearings should be reformed. We review the two main calls for change—one that says senators should ask the nominees fewer substantive questions, and the other that says they should ask them more. Our findings, we believe, highlight at least three reasons why these proposals have not yet met with much success. Most notably, we argue that by focusing too intently on the post-Bork nominees, critics have failed to appreciate that whatever problems the hearings might have are inherent in the process. Moreover, by vastly overestimating the degree to which the post-Bork nominees have been evasive, these same critics have suggested changes that are too sweeping. Instead, we suggest a more modest solution that allows senators to use the kinds of findings we present in this book to assess nominees against an objective standard of responsiveness.

Ultimately, whether this proposal is put to use or not, we think that the findings outlined in this book represent an important challenge to the longstanding belief that Supreme Court confirmation hearings have become a vapid and hollow charade in recent years. But this is more than just an academic debate: as noted above, we think that this misperception about the hearings has very real consequences for the Court and the country. It affects how the hearings are conducted, what kinds of questions are asked, and how the nominees are perceived. And it affects public confidence in the confirmation process at a time when confidence in the political system is in short supply—a key issue for anyone concerned about the legitimacy of political institutions in the United States. In short, as American political myths go, this one has a particularly long and problematic reach.

To be clear, none of this is to say that the hearings are beyond reproach. They are not. But in order to have an honest and productive debate about what those changes should look like, and about the role and function that the hearings play in our democracy, we must first get an accurate picture of the hearings themselves. We believe that the empirical evidence we provide in this book does precisely that.

TWO

The Hearings in Historical Perspective

You have followed the pattern which has been in vogue since—since Bork.

—SENATOR ARLEN SPECTER, CRITICIZING ELENA KAGAN
DURING HER 2010 SUPREME COURT CONFIRMATION HEARING

Was Arlen Specter right?[1] Have nominees since Robert Bork's 1987 failed confirmation bid become increasingly evasive—remaining mum on controversial topics in the hopes that it will help secure them a seat on the Court? Specter is certainly not alone either in his perception of the hearings or in his frustration. As we discussed in chapter 1, there is a growing consensus among scholars, pundits, and political leaders that the hearings have become a "mess" over the past several decades (Carter 1988). But is this view accurate? Have these kinds of changes for the worse really taken place?

In this chapter, we begin the process of looking for answers. Our first task is to explore the hearings from a historical perspective. How and when did the hearings begin? And have there been any obvious changes—to the structure of the hearings, the kinds of questions that are asked, or the extent to which nominees answer them—since that time?

Origins

As we noted in the previous chapter, Article II, Section 2 of the Constitution empowers the Senate to give "advice and consent" to the president with regard to justices of the Supreme Court. Though there is some ambiguity about what "advice and consent" means, when it comes to Supreme Court justices the practice has always been for the president to nominate and the Senate to vote on confirmation.[2] In terms of the prevote process, however, things have evolved considerably over time.

Standing committees were introduced in Congress in 1816. The Judiciary Committee was one of these original standing committees. Initially, however, not all judicial nominations were automatically referred to the Judiciary Committee. Instead, they had to be expressly referred by a motion from the Senate. Rutkus and Bearden (2009) recount that while this arrangement was in place, roughly one-third of Supreme Court nominations made it to the full Senate without passing through the Judiciary Committee first (Rutkus and Bearden 2009, 5).[3] In 1868, however, the Senate's rules changed, essentially mandating referral of all presidential nominees to "appropriate committees" (6). This procedure, which still prevails today, does allow for exceptions. Thus, on a few occasions—such as when the nominee was a member of Congress or had been confirmed for another federal position—the nomination has proceeded to a confirmation vote directly. But the overwhelming majority of Supreme Court nominees since 1868—and all of them since 1941—have been referred to committee (6).

As table 2.1 illustrates, however, referral to committee did not mean that a nomination would have a hearing. Between 1868 and 1929, hearings were actually quite rare. In fact, only three nominees during this time period had hearings: George Williams in 1873, Louis Brandeis in 1916, and Harlan Fiske Stone in 1925.[4] What is more, these proceedings did not resemble the modern hearings with which most Americans are familiar. Williams and Brandeis did not answer questions; only adversarial witnesses appeared and testified. And while Stone did take questions—the first Supreme Court nominee to do so at a public hearing—the inquiries were limited to his role in the infamous Teapot Dome Scandal. Thus even for these three nominees, the confirmation process was not nearly as exacting as it is today. More commonly, a nominee during this period would move through without a hearing and without much delay. As just one example of this, George Sutherland, who was selected by Warren Harding to replace Justice John Clarke on September 4, 1922, was confirmed by the Senate the next day (Rotunda 1995, 126).

Even after 1929, when the Senate passed a rule making public hearings the default procedure for judicial nominations (Rotunda 1995, 127), most of the early hearings were just formalities.[5] Indeed, as table 2.1 shows, nominee testimony continued to be the exception to the rule. For example, William Douglas appeared at his 1939 hearing but was not asked any questions, while Sherman

TABLE 2.1. Supreme Court Nominees and the Senate Judiciary Committee, 1916–54

Nominee	Year	Was Nomination Referred to Judiciary Committee?	Hearing (Y/N)?	Were Committee's Final Actions Favorable?	Did Nominee Testify at Hearing?
Louis D. Brandeis	1916	Yes	Yes	Yes	No
John H. Clarke	1916	Yes	No Record	Yes	N/A
William H. Taft	1921	No	N/A	N/A	N/A
George Sutherland	1922	No	N/A	N/A	N/A
Pierce Butler	1922	Yes	No Record; Closed	Yes; Yes	No
Edward T. Sanford	1923	Yes	No Record	Yes	No
Harlan F. Stone	1925	Yes	Closed; Yes	Yes; Yes	Yes
Charles E. Hughes	1930	Yes	No	Yes	N/A
John J. Parker	1930	Yes	Yes	No	No
Owen J. Roberts	1930	Yes	No	Yes	No
Benjamin N. Cardozo	1932	Yes	Yes	Yes	No
Hugo Black	1937	Yes	No	Yes	No
Stanley Reed	1938	Yes	Yes	Yes	Yes
Felix Frankfurter	1939	Yes	Yes	Yes	Yes
William O. Douglas	1939	Yes	Yes	Yes	No
Frank Murphy	1940	Yes	Yes	Yes	Yes
Harlan F. Stone (CJ)	1941	Yes	Yes	Yes	No
James F. Byrnes	1941	No	N/A	N/A	N/A
Robert H. Jackson	1941	Yes	Yes	Yes	Yes
Wiley B. Rutledge	1943	Yes	Yes	Yes	No
Harold H. Burton	1945	Yes	No	Yes	No
Fred M. Vinson (CJ)	1946	Yes	Yes	Yes	No
Tom C. Clark	1949	Yes	Yes	Yes	No
Sherman Minton	1949	Yes	Yes	Yes	No
Earl Warren (CJ)	1954	Recess, Yes	Yes	Yes	No
Harlan–Kagan	1955–2010	Yes	Yes	~	Yes

Source: Compiled from various sources: Garrett and Rutkus (2010); Rutkus and Bearden (2009); Rutkus and Bearden (2010); Thorpe (1969).

Note: CJ stands for Chief Justice. From 1868 to 1915 there are no records of any Judiciary Committee hearings for Supreme Court nominees, though closed-session hearings were held for George H. Williams in 1873; hearings after 1929 were open to the public. Pierce Butler's first meeting was not recorded and the second meeting was closed. John J. Parker wanted to appear before the Committee, but was not allowed. Sherman Minton was the first to decline an invitation to appear before the committee. Stanley Reed and Frank Murphy testified but few details are known. William O. Douglas was present in case senators had questions.

Minton declined the Committee's invitation to appear at his 1949 hearing (129). Meanwhile, for those nominees who did testify, the question-and-answer process was not what one would expect to see today. For instance, Frank Murphy's 1940 proceeding was completed before the Committee broke for lunch; few details are known about Stanley Reed's testimony other than that it was largely a friendly and brief exchange (Thorpe 1969); and at his 1941 hearing, Robert Jackson was only asked about his past activities as attorney general of the United States, not his judicial philosophy or legal views.

On the whole, therefore, we see from table 2.1 that the vast majority of Supreme Court nominees up through the middle part of the twentieth century did not appear before the Judiciary Committee to answer questions. Since John M. Harlan II in 1955, however, every nominee has appeared and testified—an unbroken string of 30 nominations spanning nearly 60 years.[6] As such, whatever methods the Senate might have used prior to the mid-1950s, it seems clear that the approach to confirmations since that time—nominees appear before the Committee and answer questions—is here to stay. The period from 1955 through today, therefore, represents what we will call the Hearings Era.

Key Historical Events

The Hearings Era has been defined by a number of key historical episodes. In this section, we look at five of those events with an eye toward the effects that they might have had on the two key elements of any confirmation hearing: the questions asked by the committee members, and the responses given by the nominee. Our view is that it is impossible to discuss any possible changes to these aspects of the hearings—the primary focus of this book—without first reviewing some of the historical factors that helped usher in these changes.

Brown v. Board of Education

The first of these historical events was the Court's ruling in *Brown v. Board of Education* (1954). As we noted earlier, every nominee since *Brown* has had a hearing and been questioned by the Judiciary Committee—a process that was much more sporadic before this time. This shift could, of course, be a coincidence. But there are compelling reasons to think otherwise. For one, we know that when Justice Robert Jackson died in 1954, the eight remaining justices made clear that they did not want to rule on the implementation aspect of *Brown*—the case that would come to be known as *Brown v. Board of Education II* (1955)—until Jackson's replacement was seated. Aware of this, southern Democrats and others on the Judiciary Committee who opposed *Brown* saw a drawn-out Harlan nomination as a chance to stall, or perhaps even reverse, the integration process ("Eisenhower Names Harlan" 1954; "Eisenhower Scores Delay" 1955). Questioning Harlan was an obvious way to do this, giving credence to the idea that it was Dixiecrats who "invented" the confirmation hearings in response to *Brown* (Carter 2009). Whether these senators expected the hearings to become a fixture is impossible to know, but certainly the role of the Brown ruling in setting the process in motion cannot be overlooked.

It is also likely that *Brown* helped change the kinds of questions that nominees face at their hearings. As we noted above, when pre-*Brown* hearings were held, the Committee's inquiries generally targeted a specific area, such as the nominee's role in a scandal (in the case of Stone) or his prior government work (in the case of Jackson). This was hardly surprising: until *Brown*, it was not uncommon for senators to see the confirmation of Supreme Court justices in roughly the same vein as the confirmation of a postmaster general (Kamisar 1986). But *Brown* changed that perspective. If Supreme Court justices were now willing to play a more active role in political and social controversies, then senators were naturally going to scrutinize the nominations more carefully. Filling empty seats on the bench was now seen as a high-stakes political event, requiring a more searching investigation of a prospective justice's views. As such, one would certainly not be surprised to see, among other things, more substantive questioning of nominees in the post-*Brown* era.

Fortas, Haynsworth, and Carswell

Another important historical episode that likely helped shape the hearings was the failed nominations of Abe Fortas, Clement Haynsworth, and Harrold Carswell—all of which happened during a tumultuous three-year period from 1968 to 1970. Though there had been unsuccessful bids for the Court in the past, none had occurred since the Hearings Era began in 1955. As a result, the hearings provided a setting for a series of pitched political battles—something that may have helped bring a transformative new element of partisanship into the proceedings.

A brief review of the events surrounding these failed nominations helps to illustrate the degree to which they left their mark. First, in June 1968, Earl War-ren announced his retirement, allowing Lyndon Johnson the chance to name the next chief justice. Senate Republicans objected, arguing that it should be Johnson's successor—they hoped it would be Richard Nixon—who should be allowed to name Warren's replacement. Undeterred, Johnson selected Abe For-tas, an associate justice on the Supreme Court and his longtime friend and ally, to replace Warren. He also named Homer Thornberry, another ally who had actually been elected to LBJ's seat in the House of Representatives in 1948 when he became a senator, and then became a federal judge in 1963, to replace Fortas. As hearings for both nominees approached, Republican opposition—based in part on Johnson's lame-duck status and in part because of what appeared to be cronyism—grew considerably. During his 1968 hearing, Fortas faced sharp questioning about both his judicial philosophy and his relationship with LBJ. When it was discovered that he had accepted money for speeches while on the Court, his confirmation prospects were in trouble. Though his nomination was approved by the Judiciary Committee, Fortas emerged vulnerable. Republicans successfully filibustered, and Fortas withdrew his name, returning to his seat as an associate justice. This in turn forced Thornberry's name to be withdrawn, and pushed Warren to stay on the bench until after the presidential election.

This fight continued during Nixon's first term. Fortas stepped down in May 1969 because of a scandal involving his connections to a wealthy financier who had been convicted of securities fraud. To fill the vacancy, Nixon first nomi-nated Clement Haynsworth, a southerner with conservative views on racial integration and unions. Haynsworth's hearing focused largely on his past busi-ness dealings, which some senators thought raised conflict-of-interest issues, as well as his controversial views on civil rights. Nixon sought to nullify any criticism of Haynsworth by reducing it to "brutal" and "vicious" politics (Hayn-sworth 1969, 1), but the Senate nevertheless voted to reject the nomination by a vote of 55–45. A month later, in January 1970, Nixon tried again to fill the Fortas seat with another southerner, Harrold Carswell. Shortly after Carswell's name was submitted, however, it was discovered that he had made a 1948 speech in which he praised white supremacy. Democrats on the Judiciary Committee pressed Carswell on his views on race, as well as his past business dealings. Once again, the president stood by his nominee, going so far as to attack Car-swell's critics for infringing on executive authority. But Carswell's bid failed in the full Senate by a vote of 51–45.[7]

Taken together, these three hearings likely "inject[ed] politics into the confirmation fight" in a way that previous hearings did not ("Justices Not Candidates" 1968, 42). As such, if Supreme Court confirmation hearings were not always a political battleground before the late 1960s, they certainly were pushed in that direction by the clashes over Fortas, Haynsworth, and Carswell.

The Abortion Debate

The Court's decisions in abortion rights cases also have to be taken into account when evaluating the evolution of the confirmation hearing process. As David O'Brien (2011) famously and accurately described it, *Roe v. Wade* placed the Supreme Court at the "storm center" of American politics. By extension, it seems safe to say that the confirmation hearings were similarly affected.

Interestingly, however, it was not until many years after *Roe* that the impact of the abortion debate on the confirmation hearings was really noticeable. John Paul Stevens, the first nominee after the *Roe* ruling, moved through his 1975 hearing with relative ease, facing a number of questions about his position on the Equal Rights Amendment and capital punishment, but none about his views on abortion. Six years later, in 1981, abortion played only a slightly more prominent role during Sandra Day O'Connor's confirmation hearings. O'Connor began her testimony by declaring her strong opposition to abortion—a move that seemed to largely defuse concerns from antiabortion senators on the Committee. Likewise, William Rehnquist's 1986 hearings for chief justice saw almost no discussion of the abortion debate. To be sure, the Rehnquist hearings were hardly as friendly as O'Connor's, but Democrats focused much of their questioning on Rehnquist's possible role in voter intimidation efforts in the 1960s and his involvement in an anti-Jewish restrictive covenant on a property he owned in Vermont. Likewise, Antonin Scalia, whose hearings were held right after Rehnquist's, was asked a handful of questions about *Roe* and abortion, but avoided a major showdown on the issue, and was unanimously confirmed by the Senate.

Abortion figured somewhat more prominently in the hearings for Robert Bork, in 1987, and Anthony Kennedy, in 1988. But it was really not until the 1990 confirmation hearings for David Souter that the abortion debate played a dominant role. There are several likely explanations for this. Most notably, the Court's second major abortion case, *Webster v. Reproductive Health*, had been decided a year earlier. *Webster* allowed states to put new restrictions on abortions, creating anxiety among abortion rights advocates that *Roe* might soon be overturned. Those anxieties were heightened by the fact that Souter was set to replace William Brennan, a reliable vote on the abortion rights side. As such, it was hardly surprising that abortion played a bigger role in the Souter hearings than it had in previous proceedings.

It is also important to consider the possibility that the impact of the Court's abortion rulings on the confirmation hearings might have extended beyond the abortion issue itself. That is, in addition to making abortion a central issue in the hearings, *Roe* and *Webster* also may have paved the way for senators to ask questions about *other* contentious issues as well. Just as *Brown* may have broadened the scope of the Committee's inquiries decades earlier, the abortion rights cases might have had a similar effect, expanding the perimeter even further.

Bork and Thomas

It is impossible to talk about the evolution of the Supreme Court confirmation process without discussing in depth the role played by the two most well-known hearings of the modern era: Robert Bork in 1987 and Clarence Thomas in 1991. The dramatic events surrounding each nomination are familiar to most students of the Court. In Bork's case, the stage had been set for a contentious fight even before his hearing began. The Senate had flipped to Democratic control in 1986, putting any Reagan nominee in the difficult position of facing a Judiciary Committee controlled by the opposition party. Moreover, the makeup of the Court at the time was such that one more conservative vote could overturn a number of rulings that liberals considered sacrosanct, such as *Miranda v. Arizona* (which requires law enforcement to inform suspects of the constitutional right to remain silent and have an attorney or risk losing evidence) and *Roe v. Wade.* Add to this Bork's role in the Watergate scandal—he had been the one person in the Justice Department willing to carry out Nixon's order to dismiss Archibald Cox, the special prosecutor assigned to investigate the president's role in the break-in and cover-up—and it was clear to almost any observer that the White House was going to have a major fight on its hands if it wanted to get Bork on the Court. Once the hearings began, the odds for Bork became even longer: his long and candid answers to questions about his views on constitutional interpretation and issues such as privacy gave Democrats all the ammunition they needed to paint Bork as a radical conservative who would take the Court too far away from the mainstream. The Senate rejected his nomination by a 58–42 vote.

The Thomas story is even better known, though obviously for somewhat different reasons. Thomas was selected by President George H. W. Bush to replace Thurgood Marshall, the legendary champion of civil rights and other progressive causes. Concerned about the replacement of Marshall with a much more conservative judge, Democrats vowed that the Thomas hearings would be more "combative" than the Souter hearings had been a year before (Berke 1991, D18). As promised, the first set of hearings for Thomas, in September 1991, were indeed quite lively, focusing on Thomas's judicial record and his views on issues such as abortion and affirmative action. But whatever drama might have been generated by this initial set of proceedings paled in comparison to the second set of hearings a month later, where the focus was solely on the allegations that Thomas had sexually harassed Anita Hill, one of his subordinates at the Equal Employment Opportunity Commission, a decade earlier. Part political theater, part lurid soap opera, the Thomas saga transfixed the country throughout the fall, and to this day the hearings remain one of the most memorable and divisive chapters in recent American political history.

Together, the Bork and Thomas hearings seem to have brought several new dimensions to Supreme Court confirmation hearings. For one, they appear to have raised the level of partisan rancor and polarization, at least temporarily. Moreover, they introduced an element of sensationalism and drama that had not really been seen in earlier proceedings. Lastly, both hearings served as a reminder that nominees can in fact be rejected by the Senate. By the time Bork's nomination was up for a vote, it had been nearly twenty years since a confirmation had failed. Between the Bork defeat and Thomas's narrow confirmation, the message from the Senate was clear: We are not afraid to say "no" to nominees who do not pass muster.

Media Coverage

Both the Bork and Thomas hearings had another thing in common as well: they received an unprecedented amount of attention from the news media. This brings us to our fifth and final key development in the history of the hearings. Until the 1980s, coverage of the hearings was largely limited to next-day reports in newspapers. There were no live television broadcasts. As such, one could probably fit all of the Americans who had actually seen and heard a Supreme Court confirmation hearing before 1981 into a large auditorium. By contrast, beginning with the Sandra Day O'Connor hearings, all of the hearings have been carried gavel-to-gavel, on television, radio, and, more recently, the Internet. The broadcasts were at first limited to C-SPAN, and then, by the time of the Bork hearings, expanded to CNN and PBS.[8] But by 1991's Thomas hearings, CBS, ABC, and NBC had all joined in the coverage. And today they are shown in their entirety on a number of cable television networks, aired on National Public Radio, and streamed on a number of websites. In short, a safe estimate is that tens of millions of Americans have seen or heard at least parts of the hearings from O'Connor forward. Compared with the number of viewers who had seen or heard the hearings before the 1980s, the difference is profound.

Included in this vast new audience are journalists and pundits. Reporting on the hearings, which used to be limited to an article or two in the major national papers the day after a nominee's testimony, has gotten considerably more extensive. To take just one example, the *New York Times* devoted a single article to Charles Whittaker's confirmation hearings in 1957; for Samuel Alito's, nearly a half century later, there were more than thirty. Add to this all of the wire services and blogs, and what emerges is a blanket of coverage of the hearings that dwarfs the attention given to the earlier proceedings. Again, it is impossible to calculate precisely how much more extensive the reporting on the hearings has been over the past three decades, but it seems safe to say that it has been a sea change.

Exactly how the advent of televised coverage has affected the hearings is something we explore in more detail in subsequent chapters. For now, it is enough to point out just a few of the effects that one might expect to see. First, awareness of the post-1980s hearings is likely much greater than the pre-1980s hearings. Knowing detailed information about the testimony of, say, Potter Stewart would require one to have read the transcript of his hearing. By contrast, most modern Court observers—including journalists and scholars— probably watched most of Elena Kagan's hearings. As a result, there may be a tendency to think of the hearings on a timeline that starts in the 1980s, not the 1950s. Second, the increased media coverage of hearings may have had an effect on how senators on the Judiciary Committee approach the questioning of nominees. They might, for example, use the hearings as a platform to appeal to their constituents, knowing that the proceedings are reaching millions of voters. They also might be less prepared to seem sympathetic to nominees who were selected by a president of the opposing party. Finally, one might expect the nominees themselves to approach their testimony differently today than they did prior to the 1980s. For instance, the ability to watch recent hearings, and to learn from them, may make nominees today a bit cagier and more sophisticated in how they approach their testimony in front of the Committee. Concerns about appearing as though they had prejudged cases might also inform how nominees answer questions.

Changes in the Questioning Process

The precise extent to which these five events shaped the hearings is difficult to say. But what we do know with certainty is that the hearings have undergone a number of changes—both structural and substantive—since they became a regular part of the confirmation process in 1955. As we discuss below, previous studies and our own research clearly demonstrate that the hearings have gotten much longer, more structured, and more partisan over time (Epstein et al. 2006; Krutz, Fleisher, and Bond 1998; Ringhand and Collins 2011; Wedeking and Farganis 2011). What is less clear—and therefore requires us to perform a more thorough analysis—is the extent to which there have been changes in the ways that nominees *answer* those questions. Conventional wisdom says that nominees have become less forthcoming in recent years, but, as we begin to explore shortly, we have some serious questions about whether that widely held perception is an accurate one. First, though, we look at the changes in the questioning.

Number of Questions

Perhaps the most obvious change in the hearings over the past half century involves the number of questions nominees are asked by the Judiciary Committee members. It was not uncommon for early nominees to be asked only a handful of questions. For example, Charles Whittaker was asked just 17 questions during his hearing in 1957; Byron White was asked only six in 1962. Today, by contrast, the average number of questions has increased exponentially. Recent nominees such as John Roberts, Samuel Alito, and Elena Kagan were all asked roughly 700 questions each.[9]

As figure 2.1 helps illustrate, this growth in senatorial scrutiny has been steady over time. Generally speaking, the earlier the nomination, the fewer number of questions asked. This certainly fits the historical narrative outlined earlier. Beginning with *Brown*, senators appear to have taken their constitu-

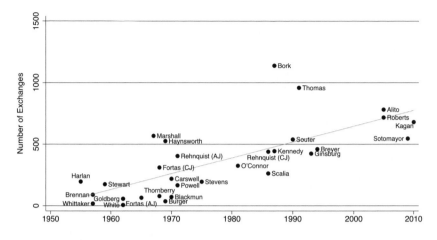

Fig. 2.1. Number of questions asked of Supreme Court nominees over time. (*Note:* Line represents best linear fit of the data.)

tional "advice and consent" duties more seriously. As time passed, the level of scrutiny increased even more—driven in part at least, we believe, by the factors we identified above: a growth in controversial rulings in areas such as abortion rights and affirmative action, a series of particularly contentious hearings, and the advent of televised coverage, which provided senators with an attractive new opportunity to serve their constituents and bolster their quest for reelection. Taken together, these factors appear to be likely explanations for the steady and dramatic increase in the number of questions that senators ask nominees.

There are a few outliers in figure 2.1. However, these too can be explained historically. The first of these is Thurgood Marshall. Until Marshall, no nominee had crossed the 200-question mark, and most were closer to 100; Marshall was asked 571 at his 1967 hearing. But this was hardly arbitrary. Marshall, the first black nominee to the Court, was bombarded with questions by Sam Ervin and Strom Thurmond—two leading voices of the southern opposition to the civil rights movement. Thurmond was particularly relentless, subjecting Marshall to a "quiz" about arcane legal issues and constitutional history (Graham 1967b, 17). Most analysts today would likely agree that the degree of scrutiny that Marshall received—unprecedented at that time—was largely because of his race.

The other most obvious outliers are Clement Haynsworth, Robert Bork, and Clarence Thomas, all of whom were asked roughly twice as many questions as the average nominee from their respective time periods. Again, there is an explanation for these deviations. As discussed earlier, these were three of the most contentious confirmation battles during the Hearings Era. Haynsworth was grilled at length by Democrats—some of whom may have been looking to retaliate for the rejection of Fortas as chief justice a year earlier—about his failure to recuse himself from a series of Fourth Circuit cases involving companies in which he was a major shareholder. Bork essentially invited intense scrutiny by his decision to engage Committee members in long debates about constitutional interpretation. And the bulk of Thomas's questions centered on the details of his relationship with Anita Hill.

These outliers aside, the picture is clearly one of steadily increasing senatorial scrutiny. In fact, bracketing the Marshall and Haynsworth proceedings, the ten longest hearings have all occurred since the early 1980s. Again, our view is that this is the result of a combination of several of the historical factors outlined above. One might counter with an alternative explanation for this trend: the Judiciary Committee has gotten bigger over time, resulting in an increased number of questions. Indeed, the overall raw size of the committee has increased, with its present day membership consisting of 19 senators compared to 15 in earlier years. Moreover, prior to O'Connor's proceedings, the norm was for less than half of the Committee members to ask questions at any given hearing. In fact, only eight out of sixteen nominees, prior to Justice O'Connor, were involved in exchanges with more than half of the senators. These results are shown in figure 2.2.[10] As illustrated, after the O'Connor hearings—the first ones to be televised—it became much more common for a nominee to face questions from the full committee. Combined with the increased size of the Committee's membership, it certainly seems possible that this contributes to the growth in the number of questions.

To assess this possibility, we measured the average number of exchanges per senator for each nominee. The results, shown in figure 2.3, clearly show an increase in this average over time—one that mimics the overall trend line in figure 2.1.[11] More precisely, the graph in figure 2.3 shows that it is not just the growth of the Committee's size or the increase in the participation rate of those senators that accounts for the increase in the raw number of questions asked. Instead, we find that, on average, senators are asking far more questions today than they did when the hearings began. Once again, this reinforces our observation that there has been a steady and significant increase in the level of scrutiny that prospective justices have received since the Hearings Era began.

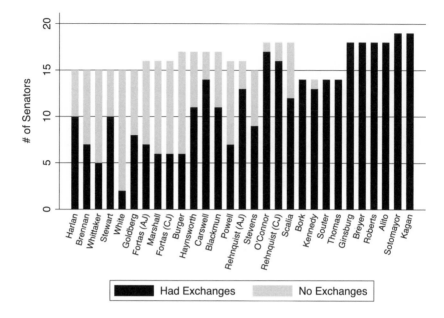

Fig. 2.2. Number of senators participating in confirmation hearings

Party Balance

Another important change in the confirmation hearings since 1955 is that the questioning has become much more evenly divided between the two parties over time. This trend is shown in figure 2.4, which tracks the percentage of questions asked by a senator who is from the opposite party of the president. As illustrated there, earlier hearings were often controlled by one party. For instance, Democrats asked 164 of the 174 questions (94.3%) during hearings on Potter Stewart (who was nominated by Dwight Eisenhower, a Republican). Sometimes this imbalance was the result of a single senator dominating a hearing, such as when Sam Ervin asked 58.9 percent of the questions put to Thurgood Marshall. Other times it was multiple senators from a single party. But as figure 2.4 demonstrates, the hearings became much more balanced—that is, the percentage of questions asked by "opposition" senators moved closer to 50 percent—as time progressed. In fact, there is a significant shift toward balance around the time of the Rehnquist hearings for chief justice in 1986.

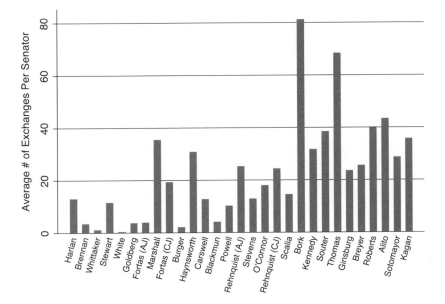

Fig. 2.3. Degree of senatorial participation in confirmation hearings

Once again, these findings match our expectations based on the historical factors outlined above. In particular, we are persuaded that the role of television and the increased media coverage of the hearings that began in the 1980s played a role in the trend toward party balance. Our view is that as the hearings began to reach a much larger audience, senators on the Judiciary Committee recognized that asking questions was an opportunity to speak to their constituents—a platform from which they could appeal to voters, enhance their overall reputation in the Senate, and demonstrate either their commitment to their party's principles or showcase their independence, depending on the circumstances. This kind of free advertising, we believe, has had a strong appeal for members of the Committee, making it exceedingly unlikely that they would pass up any chance to ask questions during their allotted time. Beyond the television factor, we also suspect that the well-documented overall increase in party polarization in Congress that began in the mid-1970s played a role here as well (Poole and Rosenthal 1984), along with the rise in partisanship in the Senate (Monroe, Roberts, and Rohde 2008). As these factors began to permeate the

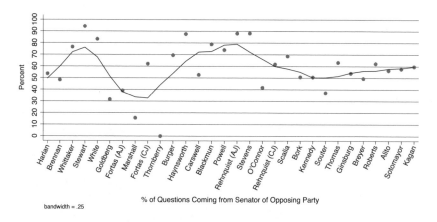

bandwidth = .25

% of Questions Coming from Senator of Opposing Party

Fig. 2.4. The evolution of party balance in Judiciary Committee questioning

Judiciary Committee and the confirmation hearings, it became much less likely that either party was going to let the other one control the hearings as they had in earlier decades. Moreover, as noted earlier, this level of partisanship within the hearings was likely enhanced even further by the three failed nominations during the late 1960s.

Types of Questions

The final major change in the hearings since 1955 is in the types of questions that members of the Judiciary Committee ask the nominees. Here we distinguish between two major types of inquiries: those that seek basic factual answers from the nominees, such as where they went to law school, and those that seek the nominees' views, such as how they approach the right to privacy. As a reminder, our expectation based on the historical events during the Hearings Era was that there would be an increase in questions about nominees' opinions over time. More precisely, our view was that as the Court moved further into controversial issue areas such as abortion, affirmative action, gay rights, and other divisive debates, there would be increased scrutiny placed on each nominee's opinions on legal matters, their judicial philosophy, or how they might rule in certain cases.

As figure 2.5 illustrates, there has indeed been a noticeable trend toward inquiries into a nominee's views and opinions—and away from basic factual

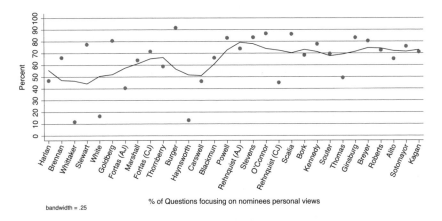

bandwidth = .25

% of Questions focusing on nominees personal views

Fig. 2.5. The changing focus of senators' questions

questions—over the past three decades. More specifically, prior to Harry Black-mun's hearing in 1970, fact-based questions were much more prevalent. Since that time—and particularly since the 1990s—the majority of the questions in almost every hearing have been directed at the nominee's views. Part of this trend is a function of an increase in questions about prior Supreme Court decisions—something that was largely absent from hearings prior to Rehnquist's 1986 hearing for chief justice (Williams and Baum 2006, 76). But other types of substantive, view-based questions have been on the rise as well (see Ringhand and Collins 2011). We theorize that this change is due, at least in part, to the fact that asking questions helps senators "score points" with constituents back home. As recent research has shown, constituents reward the party loyalty of senators at election time (Carson 2008), and since constituents pay attention during these confirmation hearings (Overby et al. 1992, 1994), constituent preferences have a renewed importance in Senate voting on Supreme Court nominees (Kastellec, Lax, and Phillips 2010). Thus, while senators have always valued ideologically laden information, it has become increasingly important in recent years, prompting senators to ask more substantive, view-oriented questions.

In later chapters, we examine whether this trend toward substantive questions has affected nominee candor and responsiveness. One might expect, for example, that a nominee is less likely to sidestep a question that asks for basic factual information (e.g., "Where were you born?") than a question that asks for her views on same-sex marriage. At the same time, it is possible that this increase in view-based inquiries has contributed to the perception that nominees today are answering fewer questions than they did in the past. For example, it may be that when questions start probing more sensitive areas, nominees deflect these inquiries in ways that call more attention to their unresponsiveness (e.g., "I cannot answer that question because it is coming before the Court soon").

Other Changes

In addition to these three major developments, there are a few other relatively recent innovations that have also helped shape the hearings. First, senators now submit written questionnaires to nominees several weeks prior to the start of the hearings. Second, since the 1970s it has been standard practice for nominees to make "courtesy calls" to each senator on the Judiciary Committee and to other senators as well (Rotunda 1995, 130). Finally, the nominee's past decisions, speeches, and other public remarks are now much more readily available to senators through television and the Internet. We believe that these innovations to the prehearing process may affect the way that senators approach questioning once the hearings begin. For example, senators who have seen a nominee's written answers on a questionnaire may use the hearing time to ask more difficult and probing questions, rather than the kinds of basic biographical questions and competency questions that the questionnaire covers. In this way, we may find that senators now come to the hearings better prepared to ask more difficult questions of the nominees. More broadly, our view is that these changes in the prehearing process have dramatically increased the amount of information that senators have about nominees before testimony actually begins. How precisely this influences the kinds of questions that may be asked is difficult to say, but it is certainly worthwhile keeping these developments in mind as we move forward in our analysis.

Changes in Nominee Responsiveness

We have just seen that during the past half century, Senate questioning of Supreme Court nominees has become more extensive, more evenly distributed among committee members, and more probing. But what about the nominees' answers? Have there been changes in those as well? The predominant view now is that today's prospective justices are more evasive than their predecessors. But is this perception accurate? Do nominees duck and dodge questions more today than they did in the past? We begin by looking in the hearing transcripts themselves for historical clues that may help us begin to answer these important questions.

Historical Evidence of Nominee Restraint and Refusals

In our initial, qualitative review of the transcripts, we found that, contrary to what the conventional wisdom suggests, nominees have actually been selectively answering questions since the hearings began. In fact, we noticed that just moments into his 1955 hearing, John M. Harlan proffered this rather stark rule regarding his testimony: "[W]ithin the limitations that are imposed upon me by the nature of the office to which I have been nominated, I will try to answer forthrightly, as directly, and as fully as those limitations permit" (135). Minutes later, Harlan put that policy into practice in response to a question about the controversial Bricker Amendments,[12] asking for the Committee's "respectful indulgence in according me what I consider to be a necessary concomitant of this high office that I should not be asked to forecast how I will decide cases when they arise before me" (139–40).

This approach did not end with Harlan, however.[13] The next nominee, William Brennan, adopted the same policy, telling the Committee that his preference was "not to discuss any matter presently pending before the Court" (1957, 18)—apparently part of his overall strategy to "win by saying as little as possible" (Stern and Wermiel 2010). Likewise, in 1959, Potter Stewart continued the practice of avoiding certain questions—a move that prompted some senators, such as John McClellan, to insist that Stewart "owes that answer to this Committee—he owes the answer to the country" (1959, 62). And in 1965, Arthur Goldberg avoided answering a number of queries that he thought were off limits. Responding to a question about national security, for example, Goldberg told the Committee, "There are several cases I have seen on the docket of the Supreme Court involving this question. If I am confirmed by the Senate, I would hope to participate in these cases. I would not like any remark of mine to lead any litigant to believe that I am prejudiced for or against any particular form of view" (9).

This selective response approach continued with the nominees of the late 1960s, and senators continued to push back. For example, at Thurgood Marshall's 1967 hearing, after a series of his questions about criminal rights went unanswered, Sam Ervin quipped, "How can the Senate perform its duty and ascertain what your constitutional or judicial philosophy is without ascertaining what you think about the Constitution?" (54). Likewise, during Homer Thornberry's testimony a year later, Ervin charged that the nominees had "virtually created a new right not found in the Constitution, which might well be designated as the judicial appointee's right to refrain from self-incrimination" (1970, 274).

Similar showdowns can be found in the hearings of the 1970s and 1980s. Although many of these proceedings were considered "friendly" (Graham 1971, 19), nominees still invoked their privilege not to answer questions on a wide range of topics. During his 1971 hearing, for example, Lewis Powell responded to a question from Birch Bayh about the role of the courts in dealing with terrorism suspects this way: "Senator, I wish you wouldn't ask me that question. I don't think I ought to speculate as to just what the Supreme Court might do, whether or not I am on it" (211). That same year, in response to an inquiry from Edward Kennedy about Congress's war power, William Rehnquist replied, "Well, I certainly understand your interest, Senator. The expression of a view of a nominee on the constitutionality of a measure pending in Congress, I feel the nominee simply cannot answer" (33). Sometimes the questions were even more direct, such as when Sen. Kennedy asked Antonin Scalia whether he intended to overrule *Roe v. Wade*. Not surprisingly, perhaps, Scalia declined to answer any query about past cases, telling the Committee, "I do not think it would be proper for me to answer that question" (1986, 37).[14] Even Robert Bork, whose 1987 hearing testimony is generally assumed to be the high-water mark for nominee responsiveness and candor, refused to answer some questions. For example, when asked for his opinion on a recent Tenth Amendment case, Bork told Sen. Chuck Grassley, "I should not speak to it even if I did know" (266).

Bork's ill-fated nomination is often blamed for making subsequent nominees much more cautious in their testimony. But as we have seen, nominees before Bork were often unwilling to answer questions. Thus the kinds of evasive maneuvers that one finds in the transcripts of the post-Bork hearings actually appear to be part of a long-standing tradition, not something new. Indeed, some of the responses look strikingly familiar.[15] Consider just a few examples, such as Anthony Kennedy's reply to a question from Orrin Hatch on capital punishment: "I have a little difficulty in answering that question because my characterization of the arguments might bear on the petition for rehearing" (1987,

115). Or David Souter's response to Herb Kohl's query about *Roe v. Wade:* "Well, with respect, Senator, I am going to ask you to let me draw the line there" (1990, 189). More recently still, pressed for his views on cases involving the Fourth Amendment, Samuel Alito told Russ Feingold: "I don't think I could answer that without providing sort of an advisory opinion about something that could well come up" (2006, 414). And in a long back-and-forth with Arlen Specter over the proper boundaries of nominee testimony, Elena Kagan advanced this justification for not answering certain questions: "You shouldn't want a judge who will sit at this table and who will tell you that she will reverse a decision without listening to arguments and without reading briefs and without talking to colleagues" (2010, 62–63).

News Coverage of Nominee Restraint and Evasiveness

In addition to these examples from the transcripts themselves, news accounts of the hearings also suggest that nominees have been selectively answering questions from the start. A review of all of the next-day articles from the *New York Times* for every hearing in our study confirms that the subject of nominee deflections has been prevalent since the proceedings began.[16] For instance, a front-page article in the *Times* devoted to John M. Harlan's 1955 hearing reported that he "declined repeatedly . . . to answer questions by members of the committee [about] how he might rule on questions involving the Constitution" (Huston 1955, 1). The next nominee, William Brennan, was also characterized as being "cautious in answering questions" (Huston 1957, 15). And the front-page article covering Potter Stewart's 1959 hearings focused on his "clash" with John McClellan over whether he should be expected to answer questions about *Brown v. Board of Education* and desegregation (Lewis 1959, 1). Along the same lines, a front-page article entitled "Thurmond Prods Fortas to Reply" reported that Abe Fortas was "forced to say approximately 50 times that he would not answer" during his hearing to become chief justice (Graham 1968, 1). Interestingly, at around the same time an article reflecting on the first decade of hearings since *Brown* characterized the proceedings as "aimless grilling" and "political flapdoodle" (Graham 1967c, 142)—a result of the unwillingness on the part of nominees to answer certain questions.

With respect to more recent nominee testimony, the same kinds of descriptions prevail. For example, the *Times* reported that Sandra Day O'Connor "deflected questions" and used "generalities" that might "hint" at her views without revealing them (Greenhouse 1981, A1), Antonin Scalia "declined to answer most of the questions in which the senators were most interested" (Taylor 1986, A1), and Anthony Kennedy "avoided some difficult issues" and "sidestepped" others (Greenhouse 1987, B16). Likewise, the headline after the first day of David Souter's testimony read "Souter Deflects Senators' Queries on Abortion Views" (Lewis 1990, A1); after his second day, Souter was described as being "more forthcoming but still ambiguous" (Greenhouse 1990, 1). Stephen Breyer's approach was described in much the same way: he was a "cautious nominee . . . keeping most answers at a level of generality that guarded against expressing a view on issues that might come before the Court" (Greenhouse 1994, A17). More recently still, John Roberts was depicted as "a profile in caution" (Toner 2005, A25), while the headline from Elena Kagan's first day of testimony indicated that she "Follows Precedent by Offering Few Opinions" (Savage and Stolberg 2010, A18).

What we see, then, is that news coverage of the hearings has always given some attention to issues of nominee candor and responsiveness, further confirming our initial impression that—from a historical point of view at least—concerns about nominees answering questions are hardly a new development. However, when combined with the excerpts from the hearings themselves that we reviewed earlier, this leaves us with something of a puzzle: If indeed nominees have been ducking and dodging questions since the hearings began, and if that tactic has been reported to the public throughout that time, then how does one account for the strong belief among Court observers that nominees have become more evasive only recently? Why is the consensus view so heavily weighted toward the view that it was Bork's fault, rather than, say, Harlan's?

One possible explanation—the most intuitive one, at least—is that while nominees have always been selective in how they answer Judiciary Committee questions, they have become *more* selective and evasive over time. In other words, while it is true that early nominees dodged some questions, perhaps recent nominees do it more often, and this is what accounts for the view that the hearings have *become* vapid and hollow. In chapters 3 and 4, we discuss how we set out to determine whether this was indeed the case, and the surprising results that we found.

THREE

Coding the Hearings

We provided anecdotal evidence in chapter 2 of nominees sidestepping questions since Supreme Court confirmation hearings began more than a half century ago. We now begin the process of performing a more systematic analysis of the hearings to determine, among other things, whether those anecdotes were simply isolated occurrences, or whether they are part of a larger pattern of nominee evasiveness. In this chapter, we discuss our methodology, focusing primarily on the detailed coding scheme that we developed to analyze senators' questions and nominees' answers. Our goal here is to allow readers to see how we made the choices that we did when categorizing the various elements of each hearing transcript. To the extent that this is the first large-scale effort to assess the hearings in this way, we think it is particularly important to outline the details of our coding scheme and to provide examples from each coding category. First, though, we explain why we focused on the period in time that we did, from 1955 forward.

Hearings

We elected to include in our analysis every confirmation hearing since Harlan in 1955. As discussed in chapter 2, some nominees had hearings before 1955, such as Brandeis, Stone, and Jackson. But as we noted earlier, those proceedings did not always boast the kind of question-and-answer dynamic that has characterized the hearings since the 1950s. Moreover, prior to Harlan, hearings were not always a part of the confirmation process, leaving gaps where several nominees were skipped. Harlan, by contrast, marks the beginning of an unbroken series of hearings that have been held for every nominee since, and as such provides us with a natural starting point for our analysis.[1]

Coding

Our initial step in the content analysis was to identify every "exchange" within each of the confirmation hearing transcripts. We defined an exchange as a question from a senator plus a response from a nominee. Most often, exchanges were easy to demarcate, as they were a single question and its corresponding answer.[2] We used the exchange as our coding unit of analysis, rather than just the utterance by the senator or just the utterance by the nominee, because we were primarily interested in how a nominee responded to a particular question, rather than each element in isolation. Below is a textbook example of a single exchange:

> BIRCH BAYH: Would you care to give us your impression, Mr. Powell, of how you feel the canons of ethics interpret substantial interest?
> LEWIS POWELL: They interpret it very narrowly. The proposed new canons, I think, use the phrase "any interest." (Powell 1971, 203)

Sometimes an exchange consisted of multiple back-and-forths because a nominee and senator were talking over each other or speaking at the same time. These were relatively few in number. For example, the following section of Justice Breyer's hearing was coded as a single exchange:

> JOE BIDEN: The second route, in this case, is for the agency to come along and say we have assembled—and I think it was about 40
> BREYER: Oh, enormous.
> BIDEN [continuing]: 40,000 pages of documentation to sustain why we think the court should make the owner clean up this site and spend an extra $9 million. But the agency did not issue an order. Is that correct?
> BREYER: That is right. (Breyer 1994, 274)

For each exchange, we noted the page number, line number, and the questioning senator, all for record-keeping purposes. The total number of exchanges from all of the hearing transcripts from Harlan through Kagan was 10,833.

Questions

Once we identified the exchanges in each hearing transcript, we turned next to analyzing the questions within each exchange. For each question, we first classified it as either a Question of Fact (QOF) or a Question of View (QOV). As the names suggest, Questions of Fact seek basic factual information, while Questions of View seek a nominee's opinions, thoughts, assessments, interpretations, or predictions. More precisely, a Question of Fact would ask a nominee for things such as names and dates (e.g., "When did you graduate law school?"); factual information about a nominee's past activities (e.g., "Did you participate in that case?"); information about whether a nominee remembers something (e.g., "Do you recall being at that meeting?"); or factual information about a past case (e.g., "That was decided 5–4, correct?"). By contrast, a Question of View would ask a nominee for their views on things such as legal issues (e.g., "Do you believe that the Constitution protects same-sex marriage?"); political issues (e.g., "Should Congress have the power of legislative veto?"); and judicial rulings (e.g., "Do you believe that *Miranda* was rightly decided?"). In short, any question that sought only facts or information was a Question of Fact; any question that asked for any kind of opinion was a Question of View.

To help illustrate these two categories, consider the following pair of questions, both of which were about past Supreme Court cases. The first, from the Haynsworth hearings, was coded as Question of Fact:

> CHARLES MATHIAS: In *Wheeler v. Durham Board of Education*, the court voided boundaries drawn with an intent to perpetuate segregation. Did you vote with the majority in that case? (Haynsworth 1969, 308)

The second, from Rehnquist's hearings for associate justice, was a Question of View:

> BAYH: Do you concur in the general concept related in *Griswold v. Connecticut* back in 1965 as the way they describe this right, the broad basis of it? (Rehnquist 1971, 164)

As these examples show, the deciding factor was not the topic of the question, but rather the kind of information being sought. Thus, along the same lines, a question that asked the nominee where they delivered a speech about civil rights would be a Question of Fact, but if the questioning turned to whether the nominee still believed what he said in that speech, it would be a Question of View.

Why did we differentiate the questions in this way? Our thinking was simple: questions seeking benign factual information are more likely to be answered in a forthcoming manner than questions seeking opinions, which could potentially derail a nominee's confirmation bid. As such, we wanted to be sure that when we analyzed the responses later, we would be able to separate the "easy" questions from the "hard" ones. Overall, we found that this distinction was not difficult to make; very few were borderline cases.

Both categories of question were then coded according to the subject or topic of the question. For Questions of Fact, the categories were: (1) legal education; (2) biography or family; (3) nonlegal employment history; and (4) nominee's writings, speeches, previous testimony, and other issues that did not fit into the first three main categories. For Questions of View, the categories were: (1) past Supreme Court rulings or a lower court ruling; (2) hypothetical cases; (3) approach to judging and constitutional interpretation; (4) powers of Congress and the president; (5) federalism and states' rights; (6) judicial power and administration; (7) peace, security, law and order; (8) individual rights and liberties; (9) other topics not identified above. Questions that cover more than one issue were coded with the main topic first, followed by secondary topics, if any.

Responses

The next part of our analysis focused on the nominee responses within each exchange. We developed a method for coding the degree to which each answer was forthcoming—allowing us to generate, for the first time, an empirically grounded assessment of Supreme Court nominee responsiveness. We also developed a second set of variables for those responses that were not forthcoming, where we coded the reasons that nominees gave for not answering the question more completely.

First, with respect to the "forthcomingness" of the responses, we constructed five categories: (1) Forthcoming; (2) Qualified; (3) Not Forthcoming;

(4) Interrupted; and (5) Non-Answers. To help understand these crucial categories, we pause here to say a few words about each and offer examples.

Forthcoming Responses

A response was classified as "Forthcoming" when a nominee answered a question directly, without offering any caveats, provisos, or qualifications. In other words, the nominee answered without hesitation, offering no indication that they had any reservations or problems with doing so. Forthcoming responses could be to either Questions of Fact or Questions of View. Here are some examples of exchanges where the answer was categorized as Forthcoming. The first is from the hearings for Arthur Goldberg:

> ROMAN HRUSKA: From the list of types of cases you have cited, it would appear that you in your practice have engaged in all aspects of litigation, administrative law, appellate work, presumably, equity work, and also jury work, and trials in all of those categories. Am I correct in that assumption?
> GOLDBERG: You are entirely correct. My practice from 1929 on ranged over the whole panoply of law. (Goldberg 1962, 12)

Such questions spanned the entire range of the hearings:

> ARLEN SPECTER: Do you agree with Justice O'Connor's statement quoted frequently yesterday from *Hamdi* that, "We have long since made clear that a state of war is not a blank check for the President when it comes to the rights of the Nation's citizens," when she was citing the *Youngstown* case? Do you agree with that?
> ALITO: Absolutely. That's a very important principle. Our Constitution applies in times of peace and in times of war, and it protects the rights of Americans under all circumstances. (Alito 2006, 324)

Note that Forthcoming answers need not be long answers. They often were long, but just as often they were as short (or even shorter) than the examples given here. The key for us in coding was not whether the answer was exhaustive, but rather whether there was any sort of resistance on the part of the nominee to answering. When such hesitation or qualification was absent, the answer was classified as Forthcoming, even if it was as simple as a single-word response, such as "No."

Qualified Responses

Our next category was Qualified Responses. These were answers where the nominee indicated that they would not be able to answer the question fully for some given reason. Instead, they gave a partial response, framed within a set of qualifications. Most commonly (as we discuss in more detail below), these "qualifications" were either that (a) they did not think it was appropriate to answer the question fully, or (b) they did not have enough information or knowledge to say more about it. Consider the following examples, the first of which comes from the Thomas hearings:

> SPECTER: Did Professor Hill not get a promotion that she was working for within your staff?
>
> THOMAS: Again, I can't remember the exact details of it, but I think she wanted to have that position, the executive assistant position. But that's again, Senator, that is speculation as to what the motivation would be and I hesitate to even mention it here. (Thomas 1991, 264–65)

Or this exchange from the Warren Burger hearings:

> MILLARD TYDINGS: Judge Burger, do you feel that a judge should assume the role of chief judge of a circuit court or a chief judge of a district court after he passes the age of 65?
>
> BURGER: Well, I do not think I am qualified really to pick a fixed age. I think there certainly is much to be said for limitations. And the Congress created the limitation about 10 years ago at age 70. At that time I think some of the proposals were to make it 65, and the compromise was made on 70. I do not have a firm view on it. I really cannot go beyond that, Senator Tydings. (Burger 1969, 12)

Again, the key here is that the answer had to be short of Forthcoming, where there would be no limitations or restrictions put on the answer, and Not Forthcoming (discussed below), where the nominee did not answer the question at all. To be in the Qualified category, a response had to represent some apparent effort to answer the question, but couched within a set of limitations or qualifications. Simply put, we were looking for instances where nominees said, something to the effect, "I would love to say more, but . . ."

Not Forthcoming Responses

The next category was reserved for responses where nominees did not give even a partial answer to the question asked. Generally speaking, we were looking for instances where a nominee explicitly invoked their prerogative not to answer the question because it would not be "appropriate," or where they said they simply could not answer because they lacked information or insights. Examples help illustrate this category well. The first is from the hearings for John M. Harlan—the first hearing in our study:

> PRICE DANIEL: You believe in local self-government and the theory that we have imbedded in our Constitution and laws?
> HARLAN: Well, you are getting into a political question again—
> DANIEL: That is right, political philosophy.
> HARLAN: —which, as a judge, I have no part in formulating and I don't think I have any views that I can express on it. (Harlan 1955, 180)

The next example is drawn from Thurgood Marshall's hearings:

> JOHN MCCLELLAN: Then I take it you disagree with that philosophy of that opinion.
> MARSHALL: I am not saying whether I disagree with it or not, because I am going to be called to pass upon it. There is no question about it Senator. These cases are coming to the Supreme Court. (Marshall 1967, 9)

One final example can be drawn from the Ruth Bader Ginsburg hearings. Here, Sen. William Cohen asks Ginsburg for her views on whether the Constitution's equal protection clause prohibits discrimination against gays and lesbians.

> COHEN: What about sexual orientation?
> GINSBURG: Senator, you know that is a burning question virtually certain to come before the Court. I cannot address that question without vio-

lating what I said had to be my rule about no hints, no forecasts, no previews. (Ginsburg 1993, 323)

In recent years, Ginsburg's "no hints" response has become known as the "Ginsburg Rule," and it is now considered the paradigmatic example of modern nominees not answering questions during their confirmation hearings.

Interrupted Responses

We included a category for those responses where a nominee was interrupted prior to giving even a partial answer. Without such a category, we would have been forced to place interrupted responses into either the Qualified or Not Forthcoming groups—neither of which accurately capture this particular type of exchange. A textbook example of one of our Interrupted Responses comes from Scalia's hearings with a question by Joe Biden:

> BIDEN: How about 1969?
> SCALIA: Well, that's not 1803. All I can say is—
> BIDEN: I am really trying to get a sense of time. (Scalia 1986, 104)

Note that if Scalia had gone on to continue his answer—if the transcript had shown that he and Biden were simply talking at the same time—we would not have coded it as an Interrupted Response. However, Scalia did not finish his thought and Biden's response was punctuated in such a way to indicate an interruption. We reserved this group for responses where a senator actually stopped a nominee from continuing on to provide even a partial response.

Non-Answers

Our last category was for those instances where a nominee gave what could best be described as a "non-answer." In our view, this was something distinct from a Not Forthcoming response, where a nominee declined to answer a question. Instead, the Non-Answer category was primarily designed for situations where the nominee answered a Question of View with a factual answer. For example, if a question asked for a nominee's opinion of executive power in the post-9/11 era, and the nominee responded by saying, "Article II outlines the president's powers, and the Court has had many cases dealing with those powers over the years," this would be coded as a "Non-Answer." Here is a classic example of a real Non-Answer taken from O'Connor's hearings:

> ORRIN HATCH: Do you see any inconsistency in giving parents the right to consent but denying the similar protection or privilege to the father of the child?
>
> O'CONNOR: Senator, my recollection of the Utah statute is that it was not one that provided for parents consent but rather for notification to the parents without a consent aspect. In fact, I think that the Supreme Court in an earlier decision had held that a statute from another state which required parental consent for a minor to obtain an abortion was invalid. (O'Connor 1981, 87)

Note that Hatch was clearly looking for O'Connor's opinion about the law—making it a Question of View—but she answered by sharing factual information about the statute. Without the Non-Answer category, this would have been coded as a Forthcoming response—something we felt did not accurately capture what actually occurred in the exchange.

We also included in the Non-Answer category those instances where a nominee answered the question with a question, as Justice Souter did here in this exchange with Gordon Humphrey:

> HUMPHREY: Permit me to interrupt there. What I mean was, is there the right of one human being, acting separately, not corporately as society or government, but one human being acting separately to take the life of another, except in self-defense, when threatened by this other human being?
>
> SOUTER: Well, are you asking this as a question of constitutional law, now, not a moral, not a personal moral issue? (Souter 1990, 172)

We developed this Non-Answer category after reading a number of transcripts and recognizing that this sort of "move" happened not infrequently. Moreover, we anticipated that this category could be especially important for our analysis because it might represent an important evasive tactic for nominees. Our thinking was that nominees are likely aware that senators are constrained in their questioning time. Thus, by giving non-answers—either type illustrated above—the nominee could decrease the total number of difficult questions about their views, a subtle but important type of answer evasion.

One final comment on our response categories: They were designed primarily to identify the degree to which a response was forthcoming, not the degree to which it was honest or satisfying. This was an intentional and carefully considered decision on our part not to attempt to intuit the motivation of the nominee when answering questions—something that we frankly felt was outside the scope of an empirical investigation such as this one.[3] Thus it is entirely possible, for example, that when a nominee said that they could not answer a question because they did not know enough about the issue, they were not being honest. But for our purposes, that response was coded as "Not Forthcoming"—meaning the nominee did not come forward with an answer, irrespective of whether they could have or not.

Reasons for Qualified or Not Forthcoming Responses

If a nominee provided either a Qualified or Not Forthcoming response, we then wanted to know why. To that end, coders classified the reason that a nominee did not answer a question into one of the following categories: (1) concerns about discussing an issue or case that was before the Court or could be before the Court; (2) the issue was not a judicial question but rather one that should be handled by another branch of government; (3) nominee claimed they did not have enough information, or could not remember enough about the issue, to give more than a partial response; (4) nominee claimed they did not have enough information, or could not remember enough about the issue, to give *any* response; (5) unclear or unspecified reason.

It is important to note that the third and fourth categories above could be either sincere or strategically evasive. That is, a nominee genuinely may not know the answer to a question, or he or she may claim lack of knowledge to avoid giving damaging testimony. Since coders could not determine the nominee's motivations in these instances, we elected to code all "I don't know" answers as "Not Forthcoming." Crucially, while we acknowledge that this coding choice could have exaggerated the level of nominee evasiveness, this would have erred on the side in favor of the conventional wisdom. Moreover, we believe that this effect was marginal at most because this particular group of answers (i.e., the "don't knows" of the Not Forthcoming category) represented such a small portion of the exchanges that we encountered (282 out of 10,883, or 2.6%).

Coders and Reliability

We developed the above codebook after reading several dozen pages of transcripts from approximately fifteen nominees, and coding sample exchanges from them. Once we established that we had an operational codebook, two coders then analyzed the transcripts.[4] To ensure strong intercoder reliability, we proceeded in several steps. We began by having both coders evaluate 100 of the same exchanges from two hearings, Potter Stewart and Sonia Sotomayor, and then compared their observations. For the question type variable (Question of Fact or Question of View), there was 98 percent agreement. With respect to the more difficult variable—how forthcoming was the response—there was 86 percent agreement for Sotomayor and 78 percent agreement for Stewart. The two coders then met to discuss their coding choices and resolve any discrepancies in their respective approaches. They then proceeded to code the rest of the hearing transcripts, with the principal investigator coder handling roughly 75 percent of the transcripts, and the graduate student coder covering the rest, spread evenly over time.

When their coding was complete, we randomly chose 901 exchanges stratified across four nominees that had been coded and had the other coder record his observations. In this group there were 100 observations from Harlan, 200 observations from Haynsworth, 200 observations from Marshall, and 401 observations from Thomas. With this sizeable sample, the agreement on the key variable of response forthcomingness was 93.9 percent (kappa .8256, $p < .001$). The agreement on the viewpoint question was 96.67 percent (kappa .9318, $p < .001$). Both of these percentage agreements are much higher than the expected agreement by chance (65% and 51.2%, respectively). Moreover, the size of our reliability check appears consistent with other work using content analysis. For example, Richards and Kritzer (2002) report rates of agreement between 87 percent and 98 percent using a 10 percent sample. Althaus and Kim (2006) report 88 percent agreement for 101 randomly selected news stories out of 3,854 total stories. In sum, our key measures appear highly reliable.

With our coding scheme established and explained, in the next chapter we turn to our first substantive questions: How forthcoming are nominees, and has this changed over time?

FOUR

Are Supreme Court Nominees Forthcoming?

*The whole point here, is that nominees now, Democrat and Republican nominees,
come before the United States Congress and resolve not to let the people know
what they think about important issues.*

—SENATOR JOE BIDEN (2006)

To hear critics tell it, the story of Supreme Court confirmation hearings goes
something like this: Back in the good old days, nominees used to come to Congress and answer every question they were asked by the Senate Judiciary Committee. Then in the 1980s things changed. After Robert Bork, nominees became
much more cautious and selective in their responses, and the hearings have
suffered considerably as a result. The typical nominee today refuses to answer
any difficult question that comes their way—often invoking something called
the "Ginsburg Rule," which says that any issue that might conceivably come
before the Court, no matter how remote the possibility, is off limits. As a result,
the hearing process, which at one time was a rigorous examination of potential
justices and their views, has been reduced to a dog-and-pony show. Nominees
should take cues from their earlier counterparts and stop sidestepping tough
questions, and the Judiciary Committee should turn back the clock on the
hearings to the way they used to be.

The Biden quote[1] illustrates this story perfectly: his criticism is directed at
nominees *now*, as distinct from nominees *back then*. Unfortunately for critics such as Senator Biden, this widely accepted story may have some holes in
it. As we reveal in this chapter, our analysis of every hearing transcript since
1955 shows that nominees do not actually sidestep or evade questions nearly as
often as the media, scholars, and other Court watchers suggest. And, perhaps
even more surprisingly, nominees have not changed that much since the hear-

ings began more than a half century ago. Generally speaking, they have always exhibited about the same mix of responsiveness and restraint, whether before or after Bork. In short, our view is that the confirmation hearings have not become "vapid and hollow" in the past few decades.

Why the Hearings Have Gotten Such a Bad Reputation

Before exploring these findings in detail, we thought it only fair to start by trying to figure out why recent Supreme Court confirmation hearings have gotten such a bad reputation in the first place. After all, it seems unlikely that the conventional wisdom—namely, that the hearings have become "exercise[s] in obfuscation" since the 1980s (Yalof 1988)—is completely baseless. What might have led so many Court observers to this conclusion?

For starters, it is true that all of the post-Bork nominees have shown some reluctance to answer questions during their hearings. For example, consider this exchange between David Souter and Senator Gordon Humphrey in 1990:

HUMPHREY: If we are endowed by our creator with certain inherent rights, among which is the right to life, is it possible that we are endowed at birth or endowed by ability or endowed in the second trimester or the first or in some other nice convenient spot, or is it more logical, in your opinion, that we are endowed by our creator when we are created with such rights?

SOUTER: Senator, I am afraid that I see that as really a question that cannot be answered, without throwing a suggestion on the *Roe* issue, and I will ask to pass on that.

HUMPHREY: OK. One last question, I think I have time for one last question. Is the Declaration of Independence reduced only to Fourth of July rhetoric, or does it have some operative status with respect to interpreting the Constitution?

SOUTER: The Declaration is certainly one of the sources that we look for meaning on disputed issues. Some of the language, as you know, that is contained in the National Declaration of Independence is mirrored in our own State constitution, in its reference to rights which are not only inherent, but some of which are indeed inalienable.

HUMPHREY: And when do they inhere?

SOUTER: There again, Senator, I think you have passed that point with me. (Souter 1990, 278–79)

Souter's approach to these questions is precisely the kind of response that could help generate the negative view of recent Supreme Court confirmation hearings that has prevailed for the past two decades. And, as one can see from the following exchange between Joe Biden and Clarence Thomas in 1991, nominees continued to answer questions selectively, and senators continued to keep score:

BIDEN: Now, am I correct in presuming that you believe that the right of privacy and the right to make decisions about procreation extend to single individuals as well as married couples, the right of priva—

THOMAS: The privacy, the kind of intimate privacy that we are talking about, I think.

BIDEN: The right about specifically procreation.

THOMAS: Yes, procreation that we are talking about, I think the Court extended in *Eisenstadt v. Baird* to nonmarried individuals.

BIDEN: Well, that is a very skillful answer, Judge. . . . Judge Souter waltzed away from that by pointing out it was an equal protection case. So that I want to know from you, do single individuals, not married couples alone, have a right of privacy residing in the 14th amendment liberty clause?

THOMAS: Senator, the courts have never decided that, and I don't know of a case that has decided that explicit point. *Eisenstadt* was, of course, decided as an equal protection case and—

BIDEN: Not alone, but go on.

THOMAS: My answer to you is I cannot sit here and decide that. I don't know.

BIDEN: Judge, why can't you? That case is an old case. I know of no challenge before the Court on the use of contraceptives by an individual. I can see no reasonable prospect there is going to be any challenge. And, Judge, are you telling me that may come before you? Is that the argument you are going to give me?

THOMAS: Well, I am saying that I think that for a judge to sit here without the benefit of arguments and briefs, et cetera, and without the benefit of precedent, I don't think anyone could decide that.

BIDEN: Well, Judge, I think that is the most unartful dodge that I have heard, but let me go on. (Thomas 1991, 277–78)

Biden's "unartful dodge" quip betrays his frustration with Thomas and with the confirmation process more generally. Indeed, after the Thomas hearings concluded, Biden even indicated that he wanted to hold hearings with lawyers and political scientists to explore possible changes in how judicial nominees are questioned, telling the *New York Times'* Anthony Lewis, "Maybe we need to set new ground rules" (Lewis 1991, 7).

But whatever changes Biden wanted to see implemented did not happen, and nominees continued to stymie senators on questions about legal and constitutional issues, as we see in this back-and-forth between Senator Larry Pressler and then-Judge Ruth Bader Ginsburg in 1993:

PRESSLER: In a recent Supreme Court decision, *South Dakota v. Bourland*, decided a month ago, the Court held that Indian tribes did not have the power to regulate the hunting and fishing of non-Indians on fee-owned land within the boundaries of the Cheyenne River Indian Reservation that had been taken by the Federal Government when it constructed a flood control project. Do you have any comments on that case and its significance in the area of tribal jurisdiction?

GINSBURG: That case is a precedent that may require interpretation in cases that will arise in the future. It would not be proper for me to comment on how that precedent will be interpreted in the next case, when the next case may be before a court on which I serve.

PRESSLER: Do you feel the Court was correct in basing its analysis of the case of *Montana v. United States*, which is a 1981 case, which held that the tribal power did not extend to the regulation of hunting and fishing by nonmembers on reservation land owned in fee by nonmembers of the tribe?

GINSBURG: Senator, I feel obliged to give the same response to that question. It calls for interpretation of a precedent likely to figure in a future case.

PRESSLER: The ninth circuit, in *Washington Department of Ecology v. U.S. Environmental Protection Agency*, held that States could not regulate the activities of an Indian tribe in operating a solid waste project, only the Federal Government can regulate the operation of such facilities on Indian reservations. Do you have any thoughts on whether an Indian tribe can be made to comply with environmental regulations of a State, whose regulations are more stringent than those of the Federal Government?

GINSBURG: This is a matter that might come before me, if this nomination is confirmed. I would have to decide it in the context of a specific case, and I can't preview or forecast my decision.

PRESSLER: The Indian Gaming Act mandates that the States negotiate in good faith with the tribes in establishing compacts regulating reservation gambling. The statute does not define good faith nor set out much direction for what is required by either party.

As you know, Indian gaming has become a controversial issue in many States. What are your views with respect to the ability of Congress to mandate that these two sovereigns negotiate in good faith, without providing significant direction to either?

GINSBURG: The Indian Gaming Act is a new and much litigated law. Cases concerning that legislation may well come before me, so at this time I am not in a position to comment on it. (Ginsburg 1993, 236–37)

Perhaps more than any other nominee, Ginsburg is credited with—or, perhaps more accurately, blamed for—injecting a new level of evasiveness into the hearings. Her self-imposed policy against providing "previews" or "forecasts," which she invokes in the passage above, has come to be known as the "Ginsburg Rule," and is synonymous with the kind of obfuscation that has saddled the hearings with the bad reputation that they have today. Whether Ginsburg deserves this ignominious recognition—or whether she was simply doing what others before her had done—is a question we address shortly. For now, it is enough to point out that nominees such as Ginsburg were not completely "innocent" when it came to deflecting difficult questions—and this practice likely is at the heart of the perception that the hearings lack substance.

The most recent nominees have certainly been guilty of sidestepping some questions as well. For example, the following exchange between then-Judge John Roberts and Senator Charles Schumer in 2004 seems to be precisely the kind of "duck-and-dodge" maneuver that concerns the critics:

SCHUMER: Do you agree with the principle that the Congress has the power under the Commerce Clause to regulate activities that are purely local so long as Congress finds that the activities "exert a substantial economic effect on interstate commerce"? In other words, can Congress regulate commerce that does not involve an article traveling across State lines?

ROBERTS: Well, that's obviously the Court's holding in *Wickard v. Filburn*, and reaffirmed recently to a large extent in the *Raich* case. But I would say that because it has come up again so recently in the *Raich* case that it's an area where I think it's inappropriate for me to comment on my personal view about whether it's correct or not. That's unlike an issue under *Marbury v. Madison* or *Brown v. Board of Education*, which I don't think is likely to come up again before the Court. This was just before the Court last year, and so I should, I think, avoid commenting on whether I think it's correct or not.

SCHUMER: This is not a recent case. This is *Wickard v. Filburn*. It is from 1942, I guess it was. It is a basic bedrock of our constitutional law, law after law, the civil rights laws of 1982 and 1965 and 1964 that you talked about previously, are based on the Commerce Clause, not necessarily on *Wickard*. . . .

.　.　.

ROBERTS: . . . The fact that it was just reconsidered and reargued last year in the *Raich* case suggests that it's not that same type of case, and that's why I'm uncomfortable commenting on it. I have gone farther than many other nominees in talking about cases like *Marbury*, like *Brown*, like *Griswold*, because I thought it was appropriate given the fact that those issues are not, in my view, likely to come before the Court again.

Here's an issue that was just before the Court last year, so I can't say that it's unlikely to come before the Court again and, therefore, I think it falls in the category of cases in which I should tell you I recognize it as a precedent of the Court. I have no agenda to overturn it or revisit it. But beyond that, I think it's inappropriate to comment. (Roberts 2005b, 262–63)

Taken together, these exchanges and others like them that can be found within the post-Bork hearing transcripts certainly help shed light on why so many Court observers view recent nominees the way that they do. But are they representative of a larger trend toward increased nominee evasiveness? Or are they simply isolated examples that have gotten more than their fair share of attention from pundits and political leaders?

Have Supreme Court Nominees Really Become Less Forthcoming?

Let us begin by examining in figure 4.1 the rates of three qualitatively different types of nominee exchanges: Forthcoming responses, Less-Than-Forthcoming responses, and Interruptions. As we explained in chapter 3, a Forthcoming response is one in which a nominee answered a question thoroughly and directly without any qualification. By contrast, the Less-Than-Forthcoming line here represents all responses that fell short of that high standard. Included in this group are three response types outlined in chapter 3: Qualified, Not Forthcoming, and Non-Answers. Lastly, the Interruptions line captures those exchanges in which the nominee was not given a chance to offer even a partial response.

Based on the conventional wisdom, which holds that the hearings have become a "vapid and hollow charade" ever since Bork, one would surely expect to see Forthcoming responses in an unprecedented free fall—or at least a precipitous decline—since the late 1980s. But as figure 4.1 illustrates, this has not been the case: Forthcoming responses have *not* in fact dropped nearly as dramatically as we had been led to believe. Instead, there has been only a mild decline since the hearings for Anthony Kennedy, and this drop-off has stabilized over the last four nominees.[2] Moreover, when one considers the rate of Forthcoming responses over the entire Hearings Era, it becomes clear that this slight Kennedy-to-Kagan decline is not only more modest than previously advertised but it is also not unprecedented. There have, in fact, been at least three separate downward trends: the first from Goldberg (1962) to Fortas's Chief Justice hearing in 1968; the second from Haynsworth in 1969 to Scalia in 1986; and the third, as noted, since Bork.

The significance of these initial findings about Forthcoming responses is, from our point of view at least, difficult to overstate. Rather than seeing the kind of dramatic recent decline in candor that we expected, what we actually found was a series of modest ebbs and flows over time. As such, the widespread and persistent criticism directed at the post-Bork nominees for turning the hearings into a "Kabuki dance" appears to be seriously misplaced.

What is more, figure 4.1 points to another, equally significant misperception of recent Supreme Court nominees. Note once again the Forthcoming response line. Even for the post-Bork nominees, it hovers in the 70 percent range, mean-

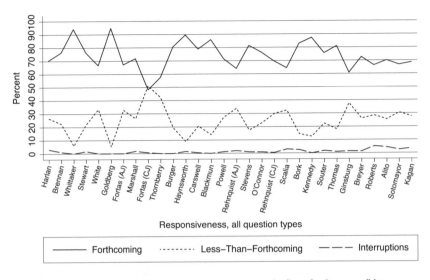

Fig. 4.1. Nominee responsiveness, all questions. (*Note:* The "not forthcoming" line comprises three categories: qualified answers, not forthcoming answers, and non-answers.)

ing that nominees answer, without any qualification, nearly seven out of every ten questions that they are asked. Thus even taking into account the modest decline in candor over the past few decades, the fact is that recent nominees are still answering a majority of their questions in a forthcoming manner. Again, this is a very different picture of nominee testimony than the conventional wisdom had led us to believe. Not only has responsiveness post-Bork been much more stable than expected but it has also been better. Thus it appears that with respect to their confirmation hearing testimony, Supreme Court nominees over the past 25 years have not been all that different—and certainly not all that much worse—than their predecessors.

Before moving on, we pause to point out two other interesting findings in figure 4.1. The first is that Fortas (CJ for chief justice) and Thornberry, the two nominees with the highest rate of Not Forthcoming responses, were not confirmed. Normally this might lead us to think that there is a correlation between candor and confirmation success. However, it is important to point out that Thornberry's name was pulled after Fortas's nomination failed (see chapter 2), and that other nominees with high levels of Not Forthcoming response rates, such as Rehnquist (AJ for associate justice), Scalia, and Ginsburg, were confirmed fairly easily. Thus we do not *yet* have any reason to draw a connection between nominee restraint and evasion, on the one hand, and confirmation prospects, on the other.

The other interesting phenomenon that figure 4.1 captures is that the line for interruptions is essentially flat and never rises much over time. Only at the very end of our timeline do we see any sort of an upward tick. This leads us to believe that while interruptions are still a very small part of these hearings, we could be witnessing a new trend where frustrated senators interrupt nominees when they are unsatisfied with their answers.

Has Outright Evasion Increased?

For all of its interesting and counterintuitive revelations, however, figure 4.1 leaves some questions unanswered. For example, we do not yet know very much about the Less-Than-Forthcoming responses. Certainly we see that, as a group, they are not nearly as prevalent as we had expected, based on the orthodox view of nominee testimony. But recall that the Less-Than-Forthcoming line in figure 4.1 represented three separate types of answers: Qualified responses, Not Forthcoming responses, and Non-Answers.[3] Thus it is possible that recent nominees have increased their rate of Not Forthcoming responses—where they basically attempt to give no information at all to a senator's query—which might help explain why they have been criticized for being so much less forthcoming than their predecessors. Figure 4.2 contains these results.

As shown, all three types of evasion generally fluctuate together, and there is no clear trend over the entire Hearings Era for any one of them. There appear to be slightly more Qualified Answers than the other types in recent years, but historically this has not always been the case. Meanwhile, Non-Answers, where the nominee gives factual answers to questions seeking opinions, appear to be experiencing a slight increase in recent years since Breyer. But in general, we see nothing in figure 4.2 that strongly suggests that one type of deflective response is dominating over any other.

What figure 4.2 *does* show us, however, is that Not Forthcoming answers are, save for a few exceptions, consistently below 10 percent. Recall that this category of response is reserved for answers where nominees openly acknowledge that they are not answering the question. It is the closest category we have to what critics would likely call "evasiveness."[4] Hence, we note that it is unusual for

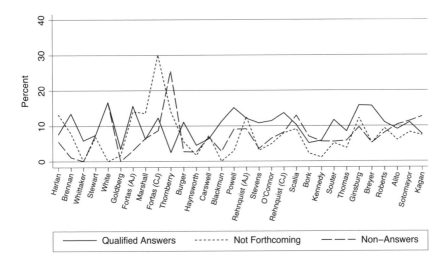

Fig. 4.2. The three types of less-than-forthcoming responses, across nominees. (*Note:* Includes all question types.)

nominees to be "openly evasive" in answering their questions—again, a finding that is at odds with what the conventional wisdom led us to believe.

In fact, what we see in figure 4.2 is that only Abe Fortas's confirmation hearing for chief justice produced a high level of outright refusals to answer. On the other end of the spectrum, of course, was Bork, who rarely gave an evasive response. Interestingly, another unsuccessful nominee, Clement Haynsworth, is also on the low end of Not Forthcoming responses. But before we conclude that failure to evade leads to problems with the confirmation vote, we should keep in mind that some successful nominees, such as Harry Blackmun, also gave very few completely evasive responses.

More significant, however, is the finding from figure 4.2 that we noted just above: the rate of Not Forthcoming answers—that is, complete refusals to respond—has been extremely low for the entire Hearings Era, including the past few decades. When combined with what we saw in figure 4.1, this latest finding gives even more support to the idea that recent Supreme Court nominees have been unfairly criticized. Like their predecessors, they generally answer the majority of the Committee's questions without qualification, and outright refusals to answer are very rare.

Why Are Some Nominees Less Forthcoming?

Thus far, we have been focused on how steady the Forthcoming line in figure 4.1 is over time—a finding that, we believe, undermines a long-standing misperception about the hearings. But now that we have effectively shown that the conventional wisdom is wrong, and that recent nominees have not driven the hearings off a cliff with their rampant evasiveness, our attention can turn to other, more complex aspects of the hearings and nominee testimony. In particular, we need to know why some nominees are less forthcoming than others. Look again at the aforementioned Forthcoming line in figure 4.1. As we have been discussing, it is higher and more stable than we had expected. But it is not altogether static. There is fluctuation among the nominees, indicating that some of them are less forthcoming than others. Can we explain why?

Recall that up until now, the answer to this question—the one we now know is wrong—was that nominees after Bork, seeking to avoid repeating his mistakes, became increasingly evasive in their responses. In other words, the "explanation" for differences in nominee response rates was, in a word, time. As we moved forward, we were told, nominees became more evasive. But we now know that this simple explanation is not an accurate one. Not only have post-Bork nominees been more forthcoming than one might have expected but some earlier nominees—that is, those *before* Bork—actually had lower response rates than their more recent counterparts. Clearly Bork's approach to his testimony cannot be to blame for this. But then how does one account for these ebbs and flows? How can we explain the variation in response rates among the nominees?

Hard Questions, Evasive Answers

We begin by examining the kinds of questions that Committee members ask. This seems to us to be a fairly intuitive idea: questions that are somehow "harder" are less likely to elicit forthcoming responses. Thus, if some nominees have gotten more of these "harder" questions than others, this might help explain the fluctuations in response rates that we saw in the previous section.

But what exactly is a "hard" question within the context of a Supreme Court confirmation hearing? Our view is that there are three particular types of questions that are more likely to trigger nominee restraint: (1) questions that focus on a nominee's views and beliefs (as opposed to questions that focus on facts); (2) questions that focus on controversial issues such as civil liberties (e.g., abortion and gun control); and (3) questions that are asked by a senator from an opposing party or by an ideologically distant senator. We examine each of these in turn.

Questions on Views

In chapter 2, we found that there was a clear increase over time in the percentage of questions seeking a nominee's views or opinions, as opposed to just factual information (see fig. 2.5). Indeed, for the last six nominees (back to Ginsburg) approximately 70 percent of the questions they faced focused on their viewpoints, or what we call QOVs, with Ginsburg and Breyer above 80 percent. This stood in stark contrast to many early nominees such as Whittaker, White, Fortas (AJ), Haynsworth, and Carswell, who were all under 50 percent in terms of QOVs. Some early nominees—Stewart, Goldberg, Fortas (CJ), and Burger— had a high percentage of QOVs, but this did not really become the norm until the hearings for Lewis Powell in 1971.

This shift toward QOVs is hardly surprising. As extensive studies have shown, ideology is a vital component of how presidents select nominees (Nemacheck 2007), and over the last 25 years ideology has become more important in explaining why senators vote the way that they do (Epstein et al. 2006; Epstein, Segal, and Westerland 2008; Krutz, Fleisher, and Bond 1998). This, in turn, explains why senators on the Judiciary Committee ask more probing questions (i.e., QOVs): it helps them gather more ideological information about the nominees. Conversely, nominees also have an incentive to resist providing ideological information because it is more likely to be used against them than perfunctory factual information. Hence, we argue that nominees will be less likely to answer QOVs than Questions of Fact, or QOFs.

Figure 4.3 illustrates this dynamic. The graph tracks the rate of Forthcoming responses for each nominee based on the type of question asked (QOF vs. QOV). For almost the entire time period, it is plainly visible that responsiveness is higher on factual questions than viewpoint questions. In fact, during the entire Hearings Era, only five nominees—and only one during the last 40 years (Rehnquist, CJ)—have been more forthcoming in answering QOVs than QOFs. By contrast, most nominees were more forthcoming when asked factual questions—some markedly so, such as Fortas (AJ) and (CJ), Marshall, Thornberry, Carswell, and Blackmun.[5] Figure 4.3 also speaks to the question of

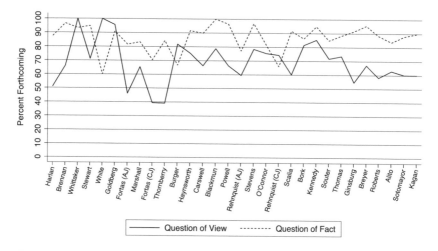

Fig. 4.3. Nominee responsiveness by question type

whether Bork's hearings were pivotal in producing subsequent change. We can clearly see that responsiveness dropped for QOVs relative to QOFs after Bork. However, a closer look shows that this divergence did not start immediately with Bork, or even with Kennedy. Instead, it appears that the lack of responsiveness to QOVs started with Souter and Thomas, and the chasm between the responsiveness lines has continued to grow since the 1990s.

As was true with figure 4.1 earlier, figure 4.3 provides us with tremendous insight into the questions that nominees answer in a forthcoming manner, but it does not tell us much about the questions that the nominees do *not* answer. For that, we offer figure 4.4, where we trace the effect of QOVs and QOFs on the three different types of less-than-forthcoming answers: (1) Qualified responses, (2) Not Forthcoming responses, and (3) and Non-Answers. These three graphs clearly show the changing faces of evasiveness over time. Most notably, perhaps, during the post-Bork era, Qualified responses rise sharply with Ginsburg and Breyer but then recede again. In contrast, we do not see any real change with Not Forthcoming answers (the middle graph), with no apparent trend in either direction. However, with Non-Answers (the bottom graph), we see a sharp increase starting with Roberts and continuing through Kagan, where they are approaching 20 percent for QOVs. In some sense, this may help explain some of the frustration captured in the quote from Senator

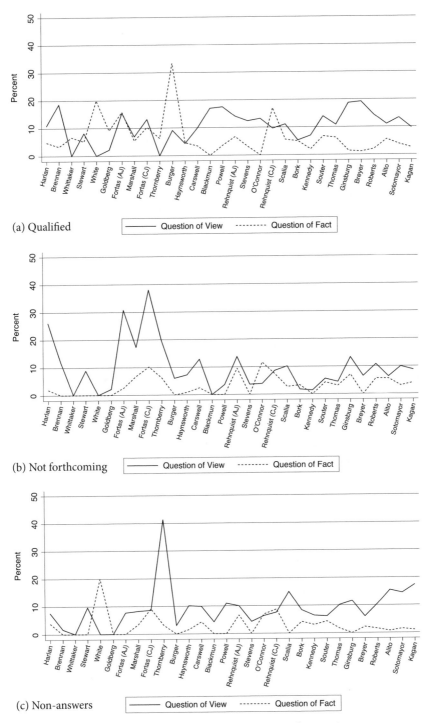

(a) Qualified

(b) Not forthcoming

(c) Non-answers

Fig. 4.4. The three types of less-than-forthcoming responses, by question type

Biden that began this chapter—namely that a nominee testified without revealing anything substantively important.

Next, focusing on the pre-Bork era, we see that sharp increases in different types of evasion are not entirely uncommon or unprecedented. For example, Not Forthcoming responses sharply increased with Fortas (AJ), remained above "normal" levels with Marshall and then sharply increased with Fortas's chief justice hearing. Shifting our focus to the bottom figure we see that Thornberry, when asked a QOV, gave Non-Answers approximately 40 percent of the time. If we combine that observation with the top figure that shows Burger giving an unusually high number of Qualified Answers to QOFs, we begin to see that the late 1960s and early 1970s were a turbulent time for Supreme Court confirmation hearings. This corresponds well with the history we discussed in chapter 2, which identified that same time period as a crucial period for confirmation hearings.

Questions on Civil Liberties

Having established that questions that seek a nominee's views are less likely to elicit forthcoming responses than those that seek factual information, we turn next to our second of three question-related variables: questions involving civil liberties issues. Here, we anticipate that QOVs that center on civil liberties issues are more likely to generate deflection and sidestepping than other areas. As with QOVs generally, questions about civil liberties issues are particularly dangerous for prospective justices, as it is this area of law that has really positioned the Supreme Court at the "storm center" of American politics (O'Brien 2011). Hot-button issues such as abortion, affirmative action, prayer in schools, and same-sex marriage all fall under this umbrella, and we suspect that nominees make an extra effort to steer clear of saying anything controversial about these topics. Indeed, to the extent that "[t]he Supreme Court nomination and confirmation process has become one of the most contentious aspects of American politics in recent years" (Johnson and Roberts 2004, 663), much of this contentiousness flows from the Court's involvement in civil liberties cases. Thus, it stands to reason that nominees will display less responsiveness (or display more evasion) to senator questioning when the questions broach the topic of civil liberties compared to other, more benign areas.

However, before proceeding, we must first look at the distribution of question topics overall, and also how the question topics have varied over time since 1955. Figure 4.5 shows two bar graphs that illustrate the distributions of the question topics overall for both QOVs and QOFs. Focusing on the QOVs first (fig. 4.5(a)), we see that four topic areas consumed almost 80 percent of the 7,166 total questions: (1) Judicial Decision Making, Constitution, and Judging (29.1%), (2) Civil Rights and Liberties (27%), (3) Past Court Rulings (both Supreme Court and lower court) (14.7%), and the (4) President and Congress (9.1%). In short, it appears that QOVs were quite focused on a subset of topics. With QOFs, however, we see the opposite in figure 4.5(b).[6]

Using the data from figure 4.5, figure 4.6 then graphs the percentages for the three most common question QOV topics for each nominee. Several things are noteworthy here. First, there is no obvious one-directional trend for the three most common topics. The topics fluctuate over time. However, since the 1970s there does appear to be a fairly consistent focus by senators on judicial decision making, the Constitution, and judging: at least 20 to 30 percent of the questions for all nominees have been in this category. Another interesting trend is that civil rights and civil liberties questions, which have remained fairly consistent over the years, reach a high watermark with the hearings of Powell, Rehnquist (CJ), and Stevens, and show only a slight decrease during more recent nominees. Finally, while focus on past court rulings fluctuated considerably during the first 20 years of the hearings, it appears to be consistently rising over the last 30 years since O'Connor—a possible side-effect of the fact that Court decisions have become more salient over the past few decades.

Although there are no overwhelmingly clear trends in terms of question topic, it is nevertheless important to see if different topics generate different levels of responsiveness among nominees. To that end, figure 4.7 plots the Forthcoming responses for the three top issue topics and combines the remainder into a fourth. Here, we see some strong evidence that question topic may be driving some of the fluctuations in nominee candor levels. For example, nominee responsiveness to questions on judicial decision making and constitutional philosophy are higher than civil liberties questions for all but three of the nominees. Furthermore, we note that responsiveness to civil liberties questions is also lower than all "other" QOV topics, which were consolidated for the figure because they did not arise that frequently. Only responsiveness to questions about prior Supreme Court and lower court decisions rank as low as responsiveness to civil liberties questions.

Interestingly, figure 4.7 also reinforces a point we have seen earlier: evasive

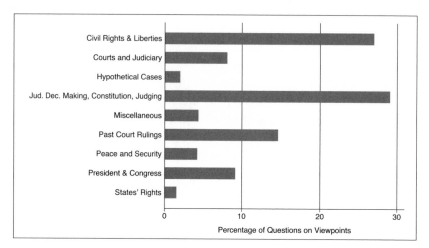

(a) Questions on viewpoints (n = 7,166)

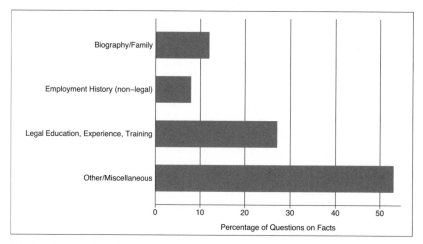

(b) Questions on facts (n = 3,713)

Fig. 4.5. Distribution of question topics for all nominees

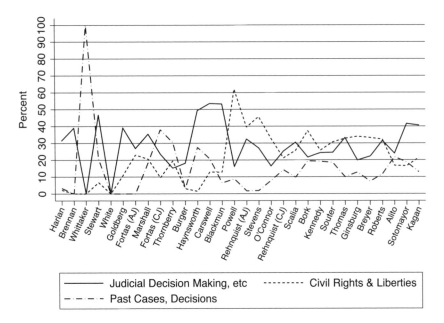

Fig. 4.6. Distribution of question topics, across nominees. (*Note:* These three topics account for approximately 70 percent of all questions.)

nominees are not a recent phenomenon. During the 1960s and 1970s, responsiveness was relatively low when nominees were asked questions on civil liberties and prior judicial decisions. This should not be surprising given that many judges routinely remark that it would be unethical for them to comment on cases that might be before them in the future or if they need to revisit an issue from an earlier case (e.g., Roberts earlier this chapter). Moreover, it should dispel any argument that suggests low levels of responsiveness are of recent vintage.

But figure 4.7 also shows us something new: responsiveness to civil rights and liberties questions, along with questions on prior court decisions, start to decline after Kennedy. By contrast, the forthcoming responses to general judicial philosophy and decision making questions, along with all "other" topics, has remained relatively consistent in their high level of responsiveness. The discrepancy between the top two lines and the bottom two lines during the post-

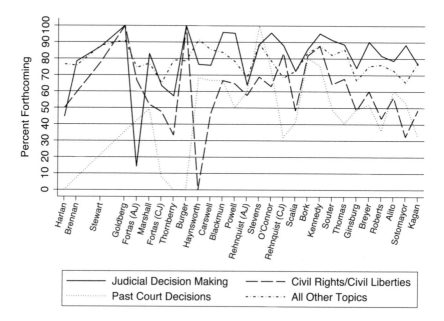

Fig. 4.7. Responsiveness, by question topic

Bork era is striking. This is an important finding because it may help explain why there is such a strong perception that post-Bork nominees have become less forthcoming. That is, even though the overall responsiveness rate has been fairly steady over time for all nominees, the post-Bork nominees are less likely to be forthcoming when faced with civil liberties questions. Since these questions tend to generate the most interest and scrutiny, evasive responses to them probably stand out more than others, fueling a perception of increased evasiveness even where there is none. We return to this theory in chapter 6. For now, we keep our attention focused on trying to figure out why some nominees are, in fact, more forthcoming than others, turning now to our third and final suspected factor: party and ideology.

Party and Ideology

Here again, our expectations are straightforward. We anticipate that nominee responsiveness will be lower for questions asked by senators who are distant ideologically from the nominee and by senators from the opposite party as the president. As we stated above, perhaps the most convincing finding in the Senate confirmation literature is that ideology is the most important factor in understanding these hearings. Moreover, as we argue more extensively later in this book, televising these hearings has changed the dynamic such that senators' questions have become more about scoring points with their constituents back home. To this extent, we think that nominees will be on high alert for senators who are potentially searching for a "gotcha" moment. Thus, we expect nominees to be less forthcoming to "hostile" senators.

Before we advance to that analysis, however, it would be helpful to see whether nominees and senators have simply grown further apart, ideologically speaking. Figure 4.8 plots the average ideological distance between the nominee and the senators asking questions on the Judiciary Committee.[7] What stands out about the figure is that there has been considerable fluctuation over the entire history of the hearings, and that the committee and the nominees from the last 20 years have not been any more ideologically distant than most. In fact, one of the more ideologically distant confirmation hearings was with Scalia, who had relatively smooth sailing through his hearings. The figure also identifies, however, several nominees who faced an ideologically distant committee and had what many observers would label a contentious hearing. Rehnquist had "tough" committees both for his associate and Chief Justice hearings, as did Bork, and these findings correspond to most conventional recounting of those hearings. Moreover, even these recent hearings were not unusual compared to hearings in the 1960s, with Fortas (both AJ and CJ) and Marshall facing distant committees. To put some perspective on these distances, consider these distances between Kagan and each respective senator: (1) Kagan and Democrat Russ Feingold (WI) is .104; (2) Kagan and Republican Tom Coburn (OK) is .80; and (3) Kagan and Republican Tom Cornyn (TX) is .401.

The additional point that figure 4.8 brings to light is that nominees and senators have not drifted apart ideologically over time. This suggests that the story here may be more nuanced. Perhaps responsiveness is changing over time due to shifts in the ideological and partisan makeup of subgroups of senators. We investigate this next.

Figure 4.9 plots the percentage of questions coming from "ideologue" senators, and, by implication, the percentage of questions from moderate senators. To generate this figure, we first identified which senators were "ideologues" and "moderates" by classifying senators relative to the mean senator from their

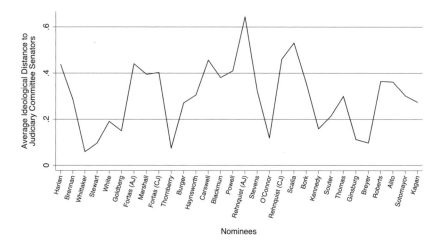

Fig. 4.8. Have senators become more ideologically distant? (*Note:* The ideological distance measure use Poole Common Space scores [Poole 1998], estimated with the procedure developed by Epstein, Segal, and Westerland 2008.)

party. Thus, if Democrats were to the left of the ideologically mean Democratic senator, they were classified as liberal Democrats. If Republicans were to the right of the ideologically mean Republican senator, they were classified as conservative Republicans. Together, these two groups, liberal Democrats and conservative Republicans, comprise the "ideologue" senators. The remaining two groups (conservative Democrats and liberal Republicans) are the "moderate" senators. As shown in figure 4.9, the volume of moderate views being exchanged at the hearings is rapidly dwindling. Ever since Burger's hearings, the percentage of questions a nominee faces from ideologue senators has increased over time. But does this have an effect on how nominees respond to questions?

To answer this question, we first examine the percentage of Forthcoming responses given to senators of the same and opposing party (of the president). Recall that we expect to see a strong divergence between the two lines, where the responsiveness to senators of the same party as the president should be trending upwards while the responsiveness to senators of the opposite party of the president should be trending downwards. The results are illustrated in figure 4.10. Strikingly, there is no significant divergence between the two lines among recent nominees. In fact, the two lines, starting in 1981 with O'Connor,

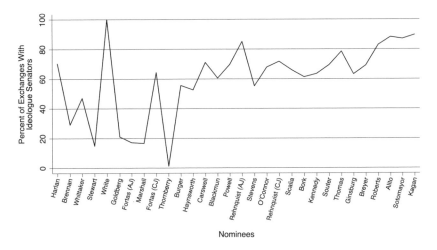

Fig. 4.9. Polarization of the Senate and questioning. (*Note:* White had only six exchanges.)

appear to be intertwined very tightly. If we step back in time, however, we do see more of a gap. Forthcoming responses to same-party senators were rather low at first (ranging from 9 percent to 20 percent), but then slowly increased over time to about 40 percent consistently for the 1980s. Likewise, Forthcoming responses to "hostile" senators was initially rather high (ranging from 40 to 70 percent), but then slowly decreased to about 40 percent from the 1970s onward.

In other words, prior to the 1980s, we see that there was considerably more variance for each nominee. What this suggests is that these hearings do appear to be settling into a "routine" of sorts, starting in 1981, and establishing somewhat of an equilibrium. Both "friendly" and "hostile" senators are treated roughly the same by nominees in terms of the degree to which they answer their questions. Later in the book, we discuss in depth the role that television, which started with O'Connor, may have played in smoothing out these differences. For now, it is enough to point out that while figure 4.10 does support the argument that responsiveness to senators has changed some over the last several decades, the change has been very modest, and we do not see dramatic partisan divergence as we would normally expect, given the increased partisanship and polarization in the Senate. The fact that recent nominees (since 1981) appear to treat senators of opposing parties in a very similar fashion suggests that nominees may be

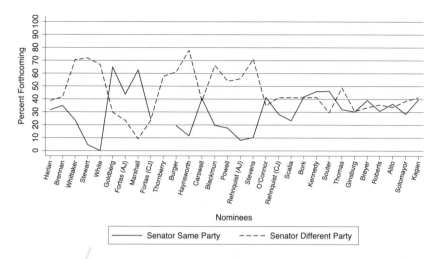

Fig. 4.10. Are there party differences in nominee responsiveness? (*Note:* Thornberry did not provide any forthcoming answers to senators of the same party as the president.)

more cognizant of their institutional status difference. That is, senators perform their constitutional duty by "checking" the other branches, which is consistent with Segal's (1987) finding that institutional politics were at least as important as partisan politics during confirmations.

Party is one thing; ideology is another. Does ideological distance have an effect on nominee candor? Figure 4.11 examines the responsiveness of nominees by plotting the percentage of Forthcoming responses to senators who are either ideologically close or distant. To determine ideological distance, we employed transformed Common Space ideology scores using a procedure similar to Epstein, Segal, and Westerland (2008), updated through the 111th Congress to include new senators and Kagan. Once we calculated a Common Space ideology score for all senators and nominees, we then calculated the (Euclidean) ideological distance between senators and respective nominees. We then used this distance measure to divide the observations into two groups: those above the mean ideological distance split (what we will call "distant senators"), and those below the mean ("close senators"). Our thinking here was that senators who are more similar ideologically to a nominee will ask questions that a nominee would find more suitable to give a Forthcoming answer.

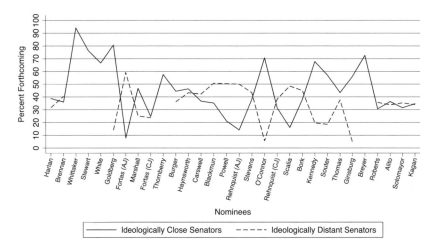

Fig. 4.11. Are there ideological differences in nominee responsiveness? (*Note:* Breyer, Whittaker, Stewart, Thornberry, and White did not give any "forthcoming" answers to distant senators. Breyer did not have any distant senators, but the other four answered questions from distant senators, just not in a forthcoming manner.)

The results illustrated in figure 4.11 are somewhat mixed. On the one hand, the recent nominees (Roberts through Kagan) are almost indistinguishable from each other. On the other hand, there appears to be a sizeable gap between the two lines starting with Kennedy and extending through Ginsburg. But prior to that, we do not see many instances where forthcomingness is more prevalent for ideologically close senators. O'Connor and Goldberg are the only nominees prior to 1986 to have a sizeable gap in the expected direction. Thus, contrary to expectations, the ideologically close and ideologically distant senator lines are similar for many of the nominees.

Taken together, the results shown in figures 4.10 and 4.11 seem to suggest that for the most recent nominees, neither party nor ideology plays a terribly important role in terms of declining responsiveness. Ideological distance played a much bigger role prior to Roberts, and party was more of a factor prior to O'Connor. Thus there has certainly been a change in recent years along these lines, and we can safely conclude that party and ideology were indeed important influences on nominee response rates prior to the 1980s. As for what changed—or, more to the point, why it changed—we return to this in chapter 6 when we discuss the role that television and other factors have had on shaping the *perception* that nominees have become less forthcoming in recent years.

Putting It All Together

Thus far we have identified a number of explanations for differences in nominee response rates, such as the type of question, the topic of the question, and the ideological and partisan makeup of the Senate. Now we test these factors more systematically with an ordinary least squares regression to see whether they withstand the scrutiny of a more stringent test that controls for many factors simultaneously. Because we are interested in nominee responsiveness, and because responsiveness varies from one senator to another, our dependent variable is the percentage of Forthcoming answers for each senator. Thus, the unit of analysis is the nominee-senator dyad, and includes observations only where a senator asked at least one question.[8]

For explanatory variables, we include measures that capture the explanations we identified earlier in this chapter: the percentage of questions focusing on a nominee's views, the percentage of questions focusing on civil liberties issues, the ideological distance between a senator and nominee, and whether the senator was of a different party than the nominating president.[9] We expect that as a larger percentage of the questions focus on a nominee's views and civil liberties, the nominee's Forthcoming response rate will decrease. Similarly, as the ideological distance between nominees and senators increases, we expect nominee responsiveness to decrease. And nominee responsiveness should decrease when nominees face senators of the opposite party of the president.

Next, we include two variables that enable us to assess the temporal trend in nominee responsiveness. The first is a time trend variable, which is simply a "counter" variable (i.e., Harlan = 1, Brennan = 2, . . . Kagan = 29).[10] The second variable is the mathematical square of the time trend variable (i.e., multiplied by itself), which allows for the time trend to have a nonlinear effect. In other words, it enables us to assess whether mean levels of candor increase during one time period and decrease during a later time period, something that the conventional wisdom suggests. A "counter" or "time trend" variable is an advantageous method for systematically identifying trends over time and has been used in other areas of political science (e.g., Cowden 2001; Palmer and

Wedeking 2011) as well as within the law and courts literature (e.g., Epstein et al. 1998; Shipan 2008).

Finally, we include several control variables that are likely to influence the responsiveness of a nominee. First, we control for the number of questions a senator asks, which we take from our earlier content analysis. Our expectation here is that more questions indicate that a certain degree of "grilling" is taking place, which in turn raises the likelihood of nominee evasiveness.[11] Next, we include a control for whether there was divided government, with the expectation that when nominees face a Judiciary Committee controlled by the opposing party, they will be forced to be more cooperative in providing answers in order to achieve confirmation.[12] Finally, we include a control for the nominees' qualifications under the assumption that more qualified nominees will be given an easier time during questioning.[13]

Table 4.1 contains the results of this analysis, which largely supports our earlier findings. Both of the coefficients for the percentage of questions focusing on a nominee's views and civil liberties result in a decrease of the nominee's

TABLE 4.1. Explaining Forthcoming Responses

	Regression Coefficients (Robust Standard Errors)
% Questions on views	−.101**
	(.055)
% Questions on civil liberties	−.149**
	(.061)
Ideological distance between senator and nominee	−13.31***
	(4.14)
Nominee different party than senator	−1.34
	(2.43)
Time trend	2.499***
	(.813)
Time trend squared	−.071***
	(.022)
Number of questions	−.037*
	(.026)
Divided government	11.02***
	(3.29)
Nominee qualifications	4.35
	(4.10)
N	342
R-Squared	.185

***$p < .01$, **$p < .05$, *$p < .1$, one-tailed test. Entries are Ordinary Least Squares regression coefficients. Standard errors are clustered on the nominee.

Forthcoming answers. Moreover, the coefficient for ideology is significant and in the expected direction, strongly predicting a lack of nominee responsiveness. We also see that when there is divided government, nominees are more likely to respond in a forthcoming manner. Moreover, our indicator for the number of questions barely reaches significance, suggesting that as a nominee is "grilled," he or she will be less responsive. Lastly, given our finding in figure 4.10 that responsiveness to both parties was largely the same for recent decades, it is perhaps not surprising that our measure of partisanship is not significant. We also note that the nominee qualifications variable has no effect.

One result worth special mention is that *both* time trend variables are significant. On the one hand, the "Time Trend" coefficient is positive, which suggests that the "average" level of nominee responsiveness *initially* increases over time. On the other hand, however, the "Time Trend Squared" coefficient is negative, which suggests nominee responsiveness decreases toward the end of the time period. Thus, nominee responsiveness has what is known as a nonlinear or curvilinear trend. Next we explore what this looks like.

Figure 4.12 plots the result of this curvilinear trend, and it reveals an important finding: nominee responsiveness increases through the 1970s, levels off starting with O'Connor, and slowly starts to decline. This is contrary to the conventional wisdom on several fronts. First, we see for the beginning period of the Hearings Era, the levels of nominee responsiveness were as low, if not lower, than in recent years. This suggests to us that perhaps some of the earlier hearings have been "romanticized." Second, this finding calls into question the prevailing view about *when* the supposed decline in responsiveness happened. Rather than starting after Bork, it started with O'Connor. And lastly, we see that the average decline in responsiveness is rather modest, dropping from about 80 percent to 70 percent with Kagan. Taken together, what we see, then, is that the average level of responsiveness has declined over the past few decades, but the rate of this decline and the timing of it are squarely at odds with what conventional wisdom has led us to expect.

Conclusion

In this chapter we set out with one major goal: to determine whether the responsiveness of Supreme Court nominees had changed in recent years, as Senator Biden's opening quote suggested. What we found was that, contrary

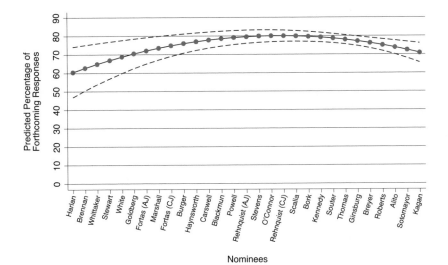

Fig. 4.12. Predicted percentages of forthcoming responses. (*Note:* Figure generated from results in table 4.1. Thornberry omitted. Dots represent predicted means, dashed lines represent 95% confidence intervals. Predictions generated with the SPost commands [Long and Freese 2006].)

to conventional wisdom, nominee responsiveness has not changed drastically over the last several decades; it has experienced only a modest decline. What is more, this decline is simply the latest in a series of ebbs and flows in nominee candor that have characterized the hearings since they began, not an unprecedented decline in forthcoming responses. We also found that the view of the earlier hearings as exercises in openness, candor, and substance is not entirely accurate. Some early nominees were quite forthcoming, but some were not.

From there, we asked: If indeed changes in nominee responsiveness are not simply a function of time—that is, if some recent nominees are in fact more forthcoming than their predecessors—then how does one explain these differences? We explored three possible factors: the types of questions being asked, the topics of those questions, and partisanship and ideological distance. Our initial analysis of these factors suggests that questions seeking views and opinions—and particularly those concerning civil liberties issues—do indeed elicit less forthcoming responses. By contrast, partisanship and ideology are less straightforward. Prior to the 1980s, both party and ideological distance appeared to play more of a role in terms of which questions generated forthcoming responses. In recent years, however, responses have been equally forth-coming no matter who has been asking the questions.

We have more investigating to do if we are going to understand fully what factors shape nominee responsiveness, and why there is such a strong perception that post-Bork nominees have been so much more evasive than their predecessors. In the next chapter, we continue this investigation by introducing a number of structural changes to the hearings that we suspect may bring us closer to understanding both of these aspects of the hearings.

FIVE

Polarized and Televised

Changes in Committee Voting since 1981

> So, for me, the first criterion upon which I will base my vote is
> whether you will answer questions fully and forthrightly.
>
> —SEN. CHUCK SCHUMER (2005)

> This was his one moment of accountability. This was the one time that almost
> 300 million Americans got a chance to ask questions before he could potentially
> take a seat on the highest court in the land. And there was too little substance
> and too little accountability to the American people and to the Senate.
>
> —SEN. PATRICK LEAHY (2006)

> I don't know how we can force nominees to be forthcoming except through our votes.
>
> —SEN. JOHN KYL (2010)

At first glance, the quotes above all point to one conclusion: Supreme Court nominees who are not sufficiently forthcoming during their confirmation hearings should not expect to get much support from senators on the Judiciary Committee. Forthcomingness, as we have been calling it, appears to be a key factor in determining whether Committee members vote "yes" or "no" on a nominee.

But a closer look at the quotes complicates things a bit. Schumer and Leahy, both Democrats, were speaking about the confirmation of Samuel Alito, who was nominated by George W. Bush. Kyl, a Republican, was talking about Elena Kagan, nominated by Barack Obama. Does this mean that senators take nominee responsiveness seriously only when the nominee is from the other party, and that they are much less concerned about it when their own party's president made the nomination? It is certainly interesting to note that in his opening statement before Kagan's hearing, Senator Schumer made none of the same demands about answering questions as he did for Roberts. Likewise, Senator Kyl's opening statement before the Roberts hearings stressed how important it was for the Committee to respect "limits on the types of questions" that were asked—a very different position from the one he took for Kagan (Roberts 2005b).

But as interesting as these quotes and statements may be, they raise more questions than they answer. Is nominee forthcomingness something that influences how senators on the Judiciary Committee vote? Is it only relevant when the nominee is from the opposing party? Or are votes really determined by partisanship and ideology in every instance—meaning that senators may talk about nominee candor publicly when in fact they are basing their decisions on very different considerations? Needless to say, we think this is an especially important set of considerations because the way that senators vote on Supreme Court nominees has profound effects on the American political landscape. Moreover, this issue goes to the heart of the claims levied against these hearings by critics. Specifically, if these hearings are not providing enough information to the senators (i.e., the hearings are broken), that poses a fundamental problem for our democracy and system of checks and balances. On the other hand, if these hearings are providing information, and yet we find that it has no bearing on how senators vote (i.e., the senators are not using the information to guide their voting decisions), then it is *not* that the "hearings are broken" but rather that the senators are using the hearings for something else. The analysis in this chapter sorts all of this out and gives us answers to these high-stakes questions.

Changes in the Senate and the Judiciary Committee

Before examining whether a nominee's responsiveness really drives how senators vote at the committee stage, it makes sense to spend a few moments discussing some of the ways in which the hearings have changed over the years. We first saw some of these changes in chapter 2, but we revisit and expand on them now in order to highlight the degree to which scrutiny of the nominees— the number of senators who ask questions, as well as the number of questions and the types of questions that they ask—has increased since the 1980s.

Senate Norms

In a 1971 law review article written on the heels of the rejection of Clement Haynsworth and Harrold Carswell, then-Senate staffer Mitch McConnell decried that the partisan body of the Senate had charted an unwise path by not providing deference to the president (McConnell 1971). According to McConnell, this regrettable development could be traced back to "attacks" launched against Abe Fortas when he was nominated to be Chief Justice in 1968 (McConnell 1971, 45). For McConnell, that kind of intense scrutiny was beyond the proper role of the Senate when it comes to advising and giving consent to the president with respect to Supreme Court nominees.

Fast forward to 2010. Shortly after Elena Kagan's confirmation by the full Senate, McConnell explained his "no" vote this way: "I voted for Breyer and I voted for Ginsburg, and I applied the standard that I had written in my law journal article in 1971 that basically the president won the election and if the person was not mediocre or obviously unqualified then we ought to have a less assertive role" (Marcus 2010). One could, of course, argue that McConnell's "no" vote stemmed from the possibility that he saw Kagan, a former solicitor general, as "obviously unqualified." But another interpretation seems at least as plausible, if not more so: senators no longer provide deference to the president when it comes to his choices for the Court.

But did a norm of deference exist at one time? And if so, how do we find evidence of it? One obvious way to do this is to see whether there have been changes in the degree of scrutiny that senators give to nominees during the hearings. Under conditions of deference, we would expect to see very little scrutiny on the part of the Judiciary Committee members. Where there is less deference (and more scrutiny), the number of questions that senators ask nominees should increase.

Figure 5.1 is a reconfigured version of figure 2.2, which showed the total number of Senate Judiciary Committee members having exchanges with each nominee. Here we display that number as a proportion of the Committee members who asked a nominee at least one question. The differences between earlier nominations and more recent ones are striking. Prior to Justice O'Connor, it was commonplace for some Committee members not to ask any questions at all. After O'Connor—and certainly after Rehnquist's associate justice hearing— the norm was for all members to ask at least one question.[1] This profound change suggests that we are likely to see other shifts in how the Judiciary Com-

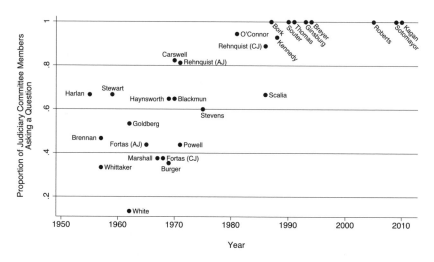

Fig. 5.1. Are nominees asked questions by all committee members?

mittee scrutinizes nominees. For example, we would expect to see a change in the number of questions that senators are asking nominees. Recall figure 2.3, which depicted how the average number of questions per senator steadily rose over the last several decades. But what if one or two senators are simply pulling the average upward by asking a lot of questions? Figure 5.2 addresses this possibility, and plots the distributions of the number of questions asked by senators as a series of box and whisker plots, one for each nominee.[2]

Figure 5.2 tells an interesting story. The distributions are shifting upward over time, gradually rising and, at the same time, becoming more dispersed or spread out. Simply put, scrutiny by senators across the board is increasing, such that today even the least active senators on the Committee register some level of participation. Once again, this shift appears to start with O'Connor. After her hearing, all nominees (with the exception of Scalia) have received a nontrivial number of exchanges from the entire Committee.

Figure 5.2 raises another interesting question: Who are the nominees and senators with the most exchanges between them? We saw a number of outlier "dots" in figure 5.2. Table 5.1 puts names to some of those dots, listing the top fifteen nominee-senator combinations for the number of exchanges. For comparative purposes, the table also lists the percentage of the nominees' answers that were "forthcoming."

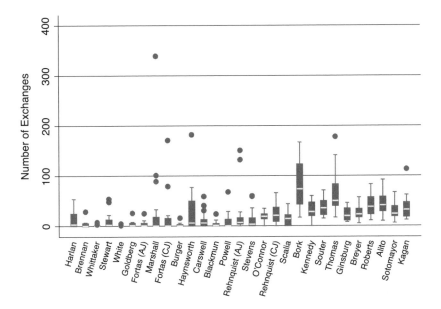

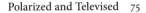

Fig. 5.2. Distribution of exchanges between senators and nominees. (*Note:* The box and whisker plots represent a distribution of the number of exchanges between senators and nominees. For example, each plot tells us the average number of exchanges from a senator, as well as more extreme senators, for each nominee. Dots represent outliers.)

At the top of the list, unsurprisingly, is the combination of Sam Ervin and Thurgood Marshall that we discussed in chapter 2—the infamous grilling of Marshall over arcane historical facts. That duo alone accounted for 339 exchanges—a number made even more striking by the fact that it occurred at a time when many nominees were asked fewer questions by the whole Committee.[3] As we also noted in chapter 2, the Marshall hearings marked the beginning of a turbulent few years for nominees. Table 5.1 supports that point as well. After Ervin-Marshall, the second largest combination is between Birch Bayh and Clement Haynsworth with 182 exchanges, 82 percent of which involved a forthcoming response.

The list is also noteworthy because several nominees appear more than once: Marshall (twice), Thomas (three times), Bork (five times), and Rehnquist (AJ) (twice). Several senators even appeared on the list twice: Bayh, Hatch, Biden, and Leahy. Once again, we also see that O'Connor's 1981 hearing marked

TABLE 5.1. Top 15 Nominee-Senator Combinations for Number of Exchanges

Nominee	Senator	# of Exchanges	% Forthcoming Answers
1. Marshall	Ervin	339	76.4%
2. Haynsworth	Bayh	182	82.4%
3. Thomas	Hatch	178	96.1%
4. Fortas (CJ)	Thurmond	171	32.2%
5. Bork	Specter	167	79.0%
6. Rehnquist (AJ)	Kennedy	151	51.0%
7. Bork	Biden	145	75.9%
8. Thomas	Leahy	141	75.2%
9. Bork	Hatch	141	90.1%
10. Rehnquist (AJ)	Bayh	132	67.4%
11. Thomas	Biden	131	83.2%
12. Bork	DeConcini	123	74.8%
13. Kagan	Graham	113	75.2%
14. Bork	Leahy	113	89.4%
15. Marshall	McClellan	101	61.4%

an important line in the sand: of the top 15 combinations listed, nine of them have occurred since O'Connor.

Notably, some of the exchanges in table 5.1 are between nominees and "friendly" senators—that is, senators who share the nominating president's party affiliation. This raises the possibility that the large number of questions in these particular exchanges represent the senator's attempt to give the nominee a chance to "rehabilitate" himself or herself by asking "softball" questions. One indication that this might be happening is if a friendly senator asks a series of factual questions, which are generally easier to answer than opinion-based questions, immediately after a hostile senator completes his or her questioning.

Consider the following examples of this sort of friendly "rehabilitation" dynamic. The first comes from Clarence Thomas's 1991 hearing. On the fourth full day of questioning, Sen. Howard Metzenbaum, a Democrat, grilled Thomas on his tenure as chairman of the Equal Employment Opportunity Commission, and on his views on gender discrimination. Metzenbaum was followed by Sen. Orrin Hatch, a Republican, who opened by reviewing several budgetary reforms that the EEOC had undertaken during Thomas's tenure. After reciting this long list, Hatch asked Thomas, "Did you work on those problems?"

THOMAS: Senator, during my confirmation hearings in 1982, one bit of advice that you gave me, indeed you told me you would hold me accountable for, was within a short period, to correct particularly the financial problems within a short period of time, and we were able to do that. In fact, we were able to correct the financial accounting problems and have a GAO certified system, I believe within 2 years.

HATCH: In fact, the EEOC had $1 million they could not even account for, is that not so, at that time?

THOMAS: That was one of the items that you told me specifically to account for in the travel area.

HATCH: And you cleared that up and resolved it?

THOMAS: We cleared that up and put in place a variety of procedures and a variety of checkpoints, so that would not reoccur. I think it would not be overstating the case to say that EEOC today has one of the finest financial accounting systems in Government.

HATCH: Is it not true that each one of those problems listed in that OPM report and listed in the GAO report, you either improved or resolved?

THOMAS: We resolved those, I believe, shortly after you instructed us to do so, as chairman of the Labor and Human Resources Committee. We attempted to address some of the long-term problems, but the recommendations that were made in the GAO report became the basis for our short-term plan, the immediate actions that we had to take upon arriving at EEOC, but most of those problems were corrected, I believe, within the first year or two. (Thomas 1991, 438–39)

This exchange illustrates the phenomenon described above, where a "friendly" senator (in this case, Hatch) asks a series of easy, largely factual questions immediately after a "hostile" senator completes his or her interrogation.

A more recent example of this sort of "friendly" senator rehabilitation comes from John Roberts's 2005 hearing. On the second day of Committee questioning, Roberts was grilled by Sen. Russ Feingold, a Democrat, on a wide range of topics, from executive power during wartime to the use of DNA evidence in criminal prosecutions. Feingold pressed Roberts particularly hard on his refusal to offer his views on specific issues that might come before the Court. As exchanges go, it was fairly heated.

So heated, in fact, that when Sen. Lindsay Graham started his questioning of Roberts immediately after Feingold had finished, he commended the nominee on his stamina, noting that "it must be 150 degrees in here" (Roberts 2005b, 266). From there, Graham offered up a series of relatively soft questions—some factual, some opinion-based—possibly in an attempt to throw Roberts a lifeline, or at least to let him catch his breath. After a short exchange about the process of selecting a Supreme Court nominee, Graham asked, "Were you proud to work for Ronald Reagan?"

ROBERTS: Very much, Senator, yes.

GRAHAM: During your time of working with Ronald Reagan, were you ever asked to take a legal position that you thought was unethical or not solid?

ROBERTS: No, Senator, I was not.

GRAHAM: We talked about the Voting Rights Act. The proportionality test in the Reagan administration's view was changing the Voting Rights Act to create its own harm. Is that correct?

ROBERTS: The concern that the Attorney General had, and the President, was that changing section 2 to the so-called effects test would cause courts to adopt a proportionality requirement, that if elected representatives were not elected in proportion to the racial composition in a particular jurisdiction, that there would be a violation shown that would have to be redressed.

GRAHAM: Do you think it would be fair to try to suggest that because you supported that position that you are somehow racially insensitive?

ROBERTS: No, Senator, and I would resist the suggestion that I am racially insensitive. I know why the phrase "Equal Justice Under Law" is carved in marble above the Supreme Court entrance. It is because of the fundamental commitment of the rule of law to ensure equal justice for all people without regard to race or ethnic background or gender. The courts are a place where people need to be able to go to secure a determination of their rights under the law in a totally unbiased way. That's a commitment all judges make when they take a judicial oath. (Roberts 2005b, 366–67)

Intentionally or not, Graham handed Roberts a perfect opportunity to rehabilitate his image as a fair and objective "umpire"—precisely the qualities he set out to showcase when the hearing began. Whatever damage the Feingold exchange might have done was probably offset by the questions from Graham that followed.

To try and understand whether rehabilitative questioning is a larger phenomenon, we checked the opening questions of senators and did not find reha-

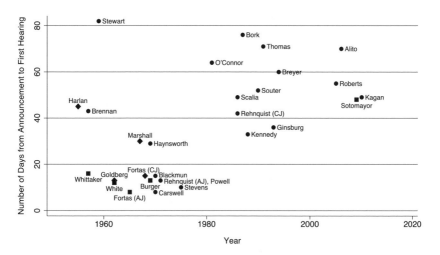

Fig. 5.3. Preparation of the Senate Judiciary Committee. (Data from Garrett and Rutkus 2010. *Note:* Brennan and Stewart were recess appointments. Roberts days were calculated from the beginning of O'Connor's vacancy. This is reasonable in this context even though Roberts technically filled Rehnquist's vacancy, the Senate had already begun preparing when O'Connor's vacancy was announced.)

bilitative questioning to be widespread or pervasive. To be sure, we think examples of them exist, but when we looked at whether senators asked nominees a series of factual questions, which are typically easier to answer, we did not find any systematic evidence that friendly senators asked any more factual questions to start questioning (assuming, of course, that rehabilitative questioning would involve multiple factual questions). Although our inquiry was tangential to our larger question and we did not want to stray too far, we do think that a more wide-ranging investigation into rehabilitative questioning would be worthy of future research.

Another way to determine whether the Senate Judiciary Committee is treating nominees differently before televised hearings is to examine the amount of time taken by the Committee to prepare for the confirmation hearings. If the time between the announcement of the nomination and the start of the hearings is only a few days, it is unlikely that the Committee members would have enough time to prepare a thorough grilling of the nominee. Conversely, senators who wanted to do serious research—opposition or otherwise—on the prospective justice would demand more than a few days. Thus we speculate that as the need for scrutiny of the nominees increases, the time between nomination and the start of the hearings will increase as well.

To test this hypothesis, we relied on the data reported in Garrett and Rutkus (2010).[4] We then graphed the number of days from the time the nominee was announced to the days of the first committee hearing. The results, illustrated in figure 5.3, are unmistakable: the Senate is taking substantially longer to prepare for the nominees since the 1980s.[5] For most nominees before that time, the Senate held hearings within 20 days of an announced nominee. Since the 1980s, by contrast, most confirmation hearings do not start until well after 40 days of a nominee being announced. Clearly, the process is slowing down—and given that the Senate largely controls this timetable, it is just as clear that it is senators who are doing the slowing.[6] Notably, scholars such as Martinek, Kemper, and Van Winkle (2002) have found a similar phenomenon taking place for judges nominated to lower federal courts as well.

The Role of Television

We have noted a few times already that most of the dramatic changes in Senate norms have taken place since O'Connor's hearings in 1981. But why would this be the case? We pause very briefly here to note simply that 1981 was the year that televised coverage of the hearings began. Thus it comes as little surprise to us that, since that time, more senators have been eager to ask questions. The hearings enable senators to engage in grandstanding, speaking to their constituents on a range of critical issues, from domestic policy to foreign affairs. Just as obviously, this gives the senators a platform to reinforce their party bona fides. If the nominee was put forward by a "friendly" party president, senators can do well by their supporting constituents by asking questions that make the nominee look favorable. If the nominee comes from the opposite party, committee members can earn points by challenging or attacking them. Either way, it seems clear that the incentive to get airtime during these hearings is very strong, and we suspect that this accounts for most of the changes we have discussed thus far. To support this point, Crain and Goff (1988) note that television increases the information available to voters, and that in states dominated by one party direct information about policy positions helps incumbents. We return to the impact of television on the confirmation process in chapter 6.

Partisanship

At the same time, the role of increased partisanship during roughly this same time period cannot be overlooked. As we noted in chapter 2, research on the Senate suggests that in the mid-1970s the parties started to polarize (Poole and Rosenthal 1984) and we also started to see a rise in partisanship in the Senate (Monroe, Roberts, and Rohde 2008). But what does party polarization look like with respect to the Senate Judiciary Committee? And more specifically, why is party polarization important for Supreme Court nominees?

To address the first question, figure 5.4 shows the average ideological value of Republican and Democratic senators on the Judiciary Committee, with the dotted lines representing the typical ideological range (one standard deviation above and below the mean). The trend is clear. The two parties on the Committee start to sharply diverge in the 1970s, and O'Connor's hearings in 1981 mark the first hearings with a clearly polarized Committee. Moreover, the distance between the average Democrat and average Republican on the Judiciary Committee in recent years is staggering.

Although these are averages, a skeptic might argue that figure 5.4 does not adequately take into account many moderate senators from each party because extreme conservative and liberal senators may be "pulling" the means apart. To address that concern, figure 5.5 shows a box and whisker plot of the senators' ideology, by party, for each nominee. Although it confirms what we found figure 5.4, the graph in figure 5.5 shows how far apart the two parties are for all Committee members. More precisely, for the nominees before O'Connor, the senators appear widely dispersed (i.e., each party is fairly spread out) and there is some overlap between Republican and Democratic senators. However, for nominees since O'Connor, not only have the parties moved further apart but the homogeneity within the party has increased as well. In other words, Republicans are now becoming more ideologically similar, as are Democrats, in conjunction with the polarization.

We pause momentarily here to see if there is a link between polarization in Congress and the perception that nominee candor started to decline in the 1980s. To do this, we first examine whether there is a correlation between nominee forthcomingness and polarization (which is defined here as the ideological distance between the average Republican and average Democrat on the Judiciary Committee). The correlation is $-.38$ ($p < .04$, $n = 29$), suggesting that as

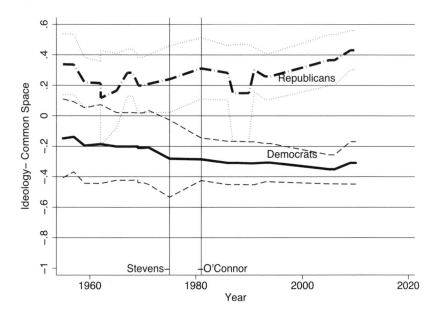

Fig. 5.4. Party polarization on the Senate Judiciary Committee. (Data from Ideology Common Space scores; see chapter 4. *Note:* Solid horizontal black lines indicate the "average" ideal point for Republican and Democrat Committee members, respectively. The dotted lines indicate one standard deviation above and below the "average" member. The two vertical lines represent Stevens [1975] and O'Connor [1981] to signify when polarization started to occur.)

polarization increases, nominee forthcomingness decreases. Next, to see if this link is tied to the perception of decline in the 1980s, we divide the observations from the first correlation and calculate two correlation coefficients—one for pre-1980 and one for 1980–2010. For the pre-1980 era, the correlation is −.27 ($p < .30$, $n = 16$), which is not statistically significant and suggests no relationship between the two. However, for 1980–2010, the correlation is −.60 ($p < .03$, $n = 13$), which is highly significant. In sum, this simple analysis confirms that polarization and nominee forthcomingness are related—though, we believe, indirectly through partisanship and ideology—and will be important as we see how televised coverage of the hearings creates a major change in the public's perception that nominees started to be less forthcoming.[7]

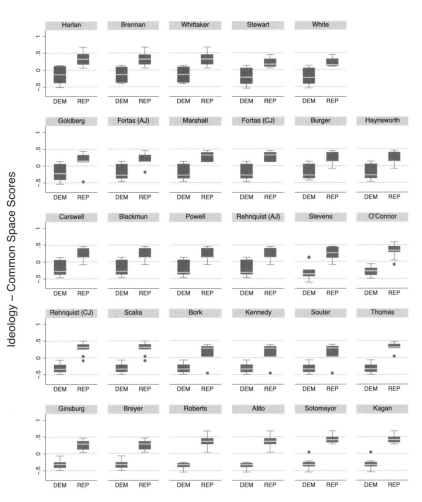

Fig. 5.5. Ideological distribution of Judiciary Committee members, for each nominee, by party

Changes in Voting

Having set the stage by illustrating some of the most important changes in how the Senate Judiciary Committee approaches Supreme Court confirmation hearings, we now can turn to the central question of this chapter: Does a nominee's responsiveness during her hearing influence how the Judiciary Committee members vote? We know from what we have seen thus far that the Committee certainly scrutinizes the nominees more extensively now than they did before the 1980s. We have also seen that partisanship in the Senate has increased since that time as well. And we also have learned quite a bit about nominee responsiveness over time. But how do all of these things affect how senators vote at the committee stage? Are senators influenced by how forthcoming the nominee was during his or her hearing? Is partisanship really the driving force? Or is it some combination of these factors?[8]

At the outset, it is important to keep in mind that the Judiciary Committee votes cast by senators based on a given motion are not formally binding on how a senator votes on the nominee on the Senate floor. Senators are free from any constraints to vote in a particular way. This leaves open the possibility that senators can vote for the nominee in Committee but against the nominee on the Senate floor, or vice versa. To some observers, this might suggest that Committee votes are irrelevant. But to the contrary, since committees are largely organized based on which party controls the Senate, how senators vote in committee is an important signal to the larger institution, and it is also something that is transmitted back to constituents in their home states. Meanwhile, others may question the validity of studying committee votes because Supreme Court nominees will not be held up in Committee, regardless of the Committee's recommendation. But here again, the committee vote is an important signal. With that said, the usual motion on which Committee members vote is to send the nomination to the floor with a favorable recommendation. If it fails, an alternative motion is offered without a recommendation or with an unfavorable recommendation.[9] Thus, the practical importance of how senators vote in committee should not be underestimated.

To start our examination of committee votes, we begin with a simple yet fundamentally important question: What are the voting distributions for each nominee and have they changed over time? In other words, have the proportion of "yes" and "no" votes changed? If there are any observable changes taking place in the voting patterns of the Judiciary Committee, this would be the most obvious place where we would see them. To answer these questions we gathered committee vote data from the Senate's official website[10] and from the *New York Times* for hearings before 1971.

The results in figure 5.6 show the "yes" and "no" votes for all 29 nominees who received Committee votes. Again, a "yes" vote means the senator favorably supports the nominee. Here we see several important trends. First, as a gen-

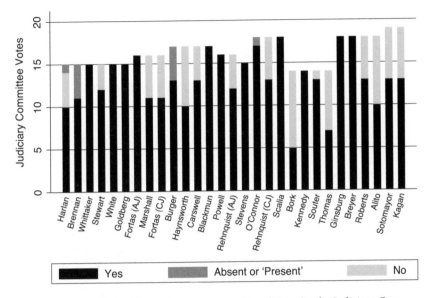

Fig. 5.6. Senate Judiciary Committee votes, over time. (*Note:* On the Judiciary Committee vote, there were two senators who voted "present," Senator McClellan for Harlan, and Senator Denton for O'Connor. There were eight senators absent for the Judiciary Committee vote. Four of the absences occurred with Burger. While newspaper accounts suggest his vote was unanimous with only one absent senator [Hart], the committee roster at the beginning of the hearings lists three additional senators; they were included as absent in the above vote totals [Senators Burdick, Fong, and H. Scott]. The other four absences occurred with Brennan, and his vote was also unanimous. While an exact source could not indicate which four senators were absent, based on attendance records we surmised that four senators never attended either day of Brennan's two day hearing [and did not ask any questions]. Thus, for Brennan, we used attendance of earlier hearings as the record of who voted, as recorded at the beginning of the hearing transcripts.)

eral matter, a "no" vote appears much more likely during recent confirmations than for the time period prior to 1981. Second, and relatedly, unanimous votes occur about twice as often during the pretelevision era (7 out of 16) compared to the television era (4 out of 13). Third, the four most recent nominees have received a substantial number of "no" votes despite indicators that suggested they were well qualified and likely to be confirmed (see Segal and Cover 1989; data updated by Segal at http://www.stonybrook.edu/polsci/jsegal/qualtable .pdf).[11]

Thus, unlike earlier nominees who ran into resistance on the Committee because of scandals or obvious shortcomings, such as Haynsworth, Carswell, and Fortas, our most recent nominees have gotten some "no" votes from the Committee despite their records. Taken together, these trends certainly seem to point to the conclusion that the era of unanimous hearings has come and gone.

Responsiveness, Partisanship, and the Vote: Testing the Hype

Figure 5.6 goes a long way toward helping us understand some of the controversy surrounding recent Supreme Court confirmation hearings. Senators no longer just defer to the president. "No" votes, even for ostensibly strong nominees, are now more common. But what we still do not know is why these senators are voting "no." As the opening part of this chapter suggested, the senators themselves often claim that it is a result of a nominee's lack of responsiveness. If true, this would have serious ramifications for the confirmation process, as it would be a strong signal to nominees that they need to answer even more questions than they do now. On the other hand, if it is not true—that is, if it is actually other factors, such as partisanship, that are driving the votes—then this would create profound implications in another direction, as it would suggest that senators are "playing the candor card," essentially using the issue of nominee forthcomingness or candor to justify their "no" vote, even though that was not the real motivation for it. This, in turn, would raise the troubling prospect that senators themselves, however unwittingly, are helping to perpetuate the myth or perception that nominees are not as forthcoming as they used to be— when in fact we now know that this is not the case.

To help untangle all of this, we conducted a multivariate test where a senator's "yes" or "no" vote on a nominee at the Committee stage is the dependent variable. The main advantage of a multivariate test, of course, is that it allows us to test the influence of many factors simultaneously. For this model, a "yes" vote is coded as a 1, and a "no" vote is coded as 0. There are a total of 463 votes total in the analysis.[12] Because our dependent variable is binary, we use logit to estimate our model, which is common practice in these circumstances.

Explanatory Variables

To explain what influences a senator to vote "yes" or "no," we have several independent or explanatory variables. Our first explanatory variable is our measure of responsiveness—the percentage of forthcoming responses that a nominee gave to a particular senator, which we described in earlier chapters. We suspect that if candor is as important as the senators' quotes at the beginning of this chapter suggest, it should be significant and positively signed. That is, increased levels of responsiveness should correspond with a higher probability of a "yes" vote, while decreased levels of responsiveness should correspond with lower probability of a "yes" vote (or a higher probability of a "no" vote). However, if nominee responsiveness is not as important a factor as senators suggest, then it should not be significant in our test. In this context, responsiveness can be thought of as a causal variable, if, as the quotations at the beginning of this chapter suggest, one considers that the very purpose of holding hearings is to extract information from the nominees. In other words, if a nominee yields a high proportion of responses that are not forthcoming, we would expect a senator to vote against the nominee.[13] We should note that included in the analysis are 122 Committee senators who did not ask a question yet still voted. The results are robust when estimated without these votes.[14]

Our second variable is partisanship. Inclusion of partisanship as an explanatory variable in congressional behavior is standard practice (e.g., Cox and McCubbins 1993). Moreover, recent research has shown that party affiliation does exert a strong influence in the Senate (Hartog and Monroe 2011). We assign the nominee the president's party, and partisanship is coded 1 if the nominee and senator are of a different party, and 0 if the nominee and the senator are from the same party.[15] If senators are basing their vote on the nominees' responsiveness this variable should not be significant. However, as our anecdotes at the beginning of this chapter suggest, and as the research on both party polarization and prior Senate confirmation voting suggest (Segal 1987), we expect partisanship to have considerable influence on the voting of senators, especially during the televised era when the parties are drifting apart (i.e., polarizing).

Next, to account for the effect of televising the hearings, we include a simple "dummy" variable, coded 1 for O'Connor's hearings through the present, and 0 for hearings prior to 1981. Additionally, based on the accounts established earlier in this chapter, we note that the effects of partisanship and responsiveness may have changed over time due to television and polarization. Therefore, to allow our analysis to test for this possibility, we include two interaction variables, which is a common method for assessing a structural change over time. The first interaction variable is between television and responsiveness, and the second interaction is between television and partisanship.

Control Variables

Our analysis also includes several control variables to account for alternative explanations. First, we control for the number of questions an individual senator asks, which we take from earlier chapters. As a senator asks more questions of a nominee, we expect the senator will be less likely to vote "yes." This makes intuitive sense: the number of questions is also a proxy for the degree of scrutiny a senator gives a nominee. If a senator is skeptical, he or she will likely ask more questions, but if he or she is supportive, then a senator will likely ask fewer questions to avoid the risk of the nominee making a mistake. Dancey, Nelson, and Ringsmuth (2011) found this to be true of lower federal court nominees. Moreover, we are further led toward this expectation by studies in a parallel area: Supreme Court oral arguments. As scholars in that area have shown, the side that faces more questions is more likely to lose the case (Johnson et al. 2009; Roberts 2005a). There, as here, questions are likely used to expose weaknesses, such that a senator looking to undermine a nominee would ask more questions.

We also control for the ideological distance between a nominee and senator, which is widely considered the most important factor in explaining a senator's vote (e.g., Cameron, Cover, and Segal 1990; Epstein et al. 2006). Moreover, some legislative scholars view ideology (and not party) as the main explanatory factor of congressional behavior (e.g., Krehbiel 1991). We use the same measure as described in chapter 4. We expect that if a senator and nominee are further apart ideologically, a senator will be more likely to vote "no." We also control for the nominee's perceived qualifications in order to account for the fact that some nominees may be so underqualified or so well qualified that they will get a "no" or "yes" vote, respectively, without consideration of party or ideology. Therefore we expect higher qualifications will result in a higher likelihood of senators voting favorably. Our source for nominee qualifications is explained earlier in this chapter. We also include a control for the presence of divided government.[16] Finally, we control for the level of interest group support. Interest group support is conceived of as the overall number of supportive groups that offered written or oral testimony, constructed by subtracting the number of opposition interest groups from the number of supportive interest groups (from Epstein et al. 2007, with the authors supplementing the source using counts for Sotomayor and Kagan).

Again, the advantage of testing these factors in a multivariate model is that it allows us to simultaneously examine whether nominee responsiveness or a senator's partisanship, or both, are affecting the votes in favor of supporting the nominee, and to see how those influences might change over time. The results of this test are shown in table 5.2. The multivariate model correctly predicts 90.7 percent of the votes, which is an improvement over simply guessing the most common outcome, which would be right 82.9 percent of the time. This tells us that the model is doing an excellent job of classifying how senators would vote, and it proportionally reduces our errors over "guessing" by approximately 45 percent. Put another way, it would be very difficult to add another explanatory variable to the model that could improve it substantially.

We can see that our measure of nominee responsiveness is statistically significant and the coefficient is positive, which tells us that as nominee respon-

TABLE 5.2. Explaining Senators' Judiciary Committee Votes

	Logit Coefficients (Robust Standard Errors)
Nominee responsiveness	.026**
	(.012)
Number of questions	−.039***
	(.007)
Ideological distance between senator and nominee	−2.92***
	(.938)
Nominee different party than senator (partisanship)	−.020
	(.664)
Divided government	−.279
	(.714)
Nominee qualifications	2.68***
	(.813)
Television-era hearing	5.20**
	(2.49)
Television × Partisanship	−4.02***
	(1.38)
Television × Nominee responsiveness	−.023
	(.020)
Interest group support	.032**
	(.015)
Constant	−.055
	(1.15)
N	463
Percent correctly classified	90.71%
Proportion in modal category	82.9%
Proportional reduction in error	45.6%

*** $p < .01$, **$p < .05$, *$p < .1$, two-tailed test.

siveness increases, senators are more likely to vote "yes." However, when we then examine the interaction variable with the television era, we see that nominee responsiveness is not significant from 1981 onward. We urge caution when interpreting logit coefficients because of the nonlinear nature of model (i.e., these coefficients cannot be interpreted in the same, direct way that the coefficients could for the model in chapter 4). Thus, to further enhance our understanding of these nonlinear interaction variables, in the section below we graph out these effects to assess whether they are significant (see, e.g., Brambor, Clark, and Golder 2006).

Interestingly, we see that our measure of partisanship is not statistically significant, suggesting that initially it has no effect on senator voting. However, when the partisanship variable is interacted with the television variable, we see it becomes significant and the coefficient is negative. This suggests that partisanship, while not significant during the pretelevision era, is significant from 1981 onward in helping explain how senators voted on nominees in committee. Moreover, this evidence is consistent with what Senator McConnell claimed earlier in this chapter: the norm of deferring to the president has declined over the years.

Many of the remaining control variables perform as expected. The variable for the number of questions is significant, suggesting that as a senator asks more questions of a nominee, he or she is less likely to vote favorably. Additionally, as the ideological distance between a nominee and senator increases, the senator is less likely to vote favorably. The nominee qualifications coefficient is significant and positive, suggesting that more highly qualified nominees are more likely to receive favorable votes from senators. This may be encouraging for observers who think the process has become too political. Yet, the evidence here still suggests that senators are responding to a nominee's perceived qualifications. Further, the overall net support from interest groups suggests that as more interest groups support the nominee relative to the number of groups that oppose the nominee, a senator is more likely to vote in favor of the nominee. This indicates that interest groups can have an important impact at this stage (e.g., Bell 2002; and Scherer, Bartels, and Steigerwalt 2008 for lower court confirmation hearings), and that the relative balance is important. Finally, our results indicate that senators vote the same regardless whether it is during a time of divided government or not.

To further enhance the interpretation of these results, we graphed the predicted probabilities for Judiciary Committee voting as a function of the level

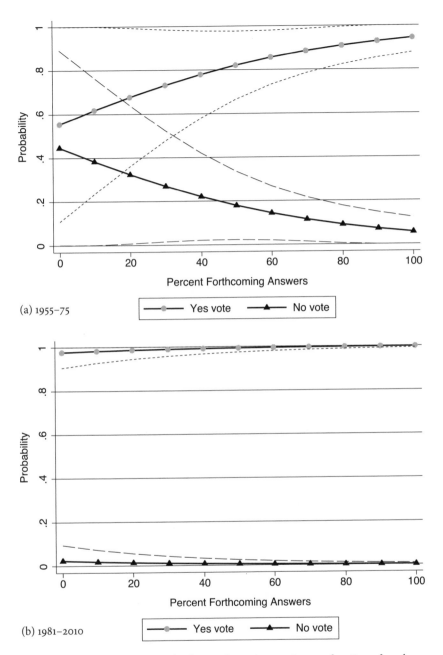

(a) 1955–75

Yes vote   No vote

(b) 1981–2010

Yes vote   No vote

Fig. 5.7. Predicted probabilities of Judiciary Committee voting as a function of candor. (*Note:* Dashed lines indicate 95% confidence intervals and solid lines indicate the mean prediction. All values were generated with the other variables set to the mean values and were generated with the SPost commands from Long and Freese [2006].)

of nominee responsiveness. Figure 5.7 illustrates how the impact of nominee responsiveness has changed over time. The solid lines represent the average or mean predicted probabilities of voting either "yes" or "no" while the dashed lines represent 95 percent confidence intervals. In the top portion, representing the nominees from 1955 through 1975, which are all nominees prior to both televised hearings and fully polarized parties, we see that nominee responsiveness clearly plays a role in distinguishing senators' votes. Specifically, when nominee responsiveness is low, ranging between 0 and 35, a "yes" and "no" vote are not statistically distinguishable from each other. However, as nominee responsiveness increases, a "yes" vote becomes increasingly more likely (while a "no" vote becomes less likely). This suggests that nominee responsiveness, at least during this earlier era, played a role in helping senators determine how to vote. However, when examining the figure for the later time period, we see that nominee responsiveness has absolutely no effect on the likelihood of a "yes" or "no" vote. Stated another way, despite the rhetoric by senators about nominees not answering questions, during recent years it does not appear to matter in terms of how senators vote.[17]

So what happened? Why is responsiveness no longer important? To answer these questions, we examine how partisanship has affected the vote. Figure 5.8 graphs the predicted probability of a "yes" vote during the different eras as a function of partisanship. Specifically, it enables us to gain some understanding of how changes in a senator's partisanship might affect their vote. The implication from figure 5.8 is clear. During the pre-TV era, before the parties were polarized, partisanship had no discernible effect on voting "yes." That is to say, a Republican senator and a Democratic senator, being roughly equal on all other factors, would be just as likely to support the same nominee. Moreover, it is also worth mentioning that the baseline level of voting "yes" is already high, at .9—a reflection of the fact that "yes" votes were, by far, the dominant action by Judiciary Committee members. Turning to the bottom two predicted probabilities in figure 5.8, we see how the effect of partisanship has changed during the era of polarized and televised hearings. In short, senators of the opposite party of the appointing president are significantly less likely to vote "yes," whereas senators of the same party as the president are almost guaranteed to vote "yes," with a probability of .99.

In short, partisan politics are alive and well during confirmation hearings in the U.S. Senate. It appears then that partisanship has displaced the previous

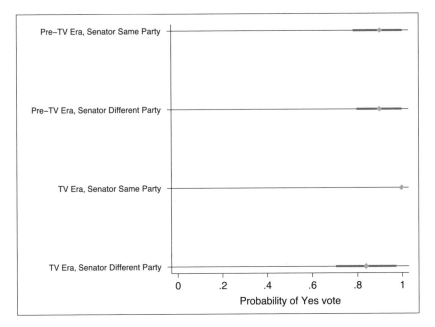

Fig. 5.8. How partisanship influences the probability of a "yes" vote. (*Note:* Dots represent the mean predicted probability and the lines represent 95% confidence intervals. Values generated with the other variables set to their mean value using the SPost commands from Long and Freese [2006].)

era's norm of deferring to the president, and that nominee responsiveness is no longer an important systematic influence on a senator's vote. Of course, it is possible that for any single senator, nominee responsiveness might be crucial in determining how he or she votes. But across the senators, at least during recent years, the results are clear: how much nominees reveal is not a systematic influence on helping them obtain a favorable vote. If anything, the results suggest the opposite. For example, while the coefficient for the interaction variable between television and nominee responsiveness in table 5.2 is relatively close to conventional levels of statistical significance ($p = .24$), because it is negative it suggests that a "yes" vote is less likely if the nominee is too responsive during the televised era. This would be consistent with the idea that the Bork hearings changed how much nominees can reveal about their own personal philosophy.

Conclusion

In this chapter, we discovered yet another piece of evidence undermining the conventional wisdom about Supreme Court confirmation hearings: senators today do not base their votes on nominee responsiveness, despite their claims to the contrary. A nominee's candor used to play more of a role, prior to the 1980s, but since then, partisan considerations have taken over. This rise in partisanship is consistent with recent research that has found that party is an important influence in the Senate (e.g., Hartog and Monroe 2011; Monroe, Roberts, and Rohde 2008). The degree to which a nominee is forthcoming is no longer consequential for how senators vote at the committee stage. This profound shift, we learned, coincides with the advent of televised coverage of the hearings as well as increased polarization in the Senate, leading us to believe that in today's institutional climate, senators are much less likely to be influenced by a nominee's testimony than they claim publicly. Whether this transfers to the full Senate confirmation vote is less clear, but we suspect that it does.

To be clear, we are not concluding that senators are being disingenuous. In fact, it is entirely possible that senators really believe that a nominee's responsiveness is crucial for determining how they vote—even though we find no systematic evidence for it in recent years. As research in the fields of judicial decision making and political psychology suggests, the factors informing decision making at the conscious level may be different from those that operate on the subconscious level—the idea commonly referred to as "motivated reasoning" (see Cross 2007, 15; Kunda 1990; Segal and Spaeth 2002, 433). Thus senators may believe they are punishing nominees for not being forthcoming when in fact they are voting against them because of partisan considerations. Whether or not this psychological analysis is in fact correct, it seems clear that senators generally see today's nominees as more evasive and cagey than their predecessors. The perception of nominee testimony is that it has become much less forthcoming in recent years. Yet as we have shown in previous chapters, this is not in fact the case.

All of this leaves us with quite a puzzle. If nominees have been roughly as responsive in recent years as they were when the hearings were just starting out, why is there such a serious misconception about the post-1980s hearings? What accounts for the widespread belief that nominees since Bork have taken the hearings into the "vapid and hollow" abyss? In the next chapter we turn our attention to this perception gap.

SIX

The Perception Gap

In chapter 5 we examined whether nominee responsiveness influences Judiciary Committee voting, testing a crucial part of our argument about the relationship between the rhetoric of responsiveness and its alleged and actual consequences. What we found was that modern senators tend to vote based on ideology and partisanship, not nominee candor—quite the opposite of what we expected to find, based on the public statements from the senators themselves, which suggested that their decisions are driven by the degree to which a nominee answers questions.

What is particularly interesting about this discovery is that it reinforces a theme that we have seen throughout this book—namely, that there is a profound gap between perception and reality when it comes to modern Supreme Court confirmation hearings. Recent nominees have developed quite a reputation—among scholars, pundits, and, apparently, senators as well—for being more evasive than their predecessors. Our work to this point has shown that this reputation is largely undeserved—that there has not in fact been a dramatic decline in nominee responsiveness or candor over the past few decades, and that some early nominees were actually much less forthcoming than some more recent ones.

But undeserved as it may be, this reputation is also extremely pervasive, enjoying nearly universal assent among scholars, pundits, and elected officials. Why? What accounts for the widespread, persistent misperception that modern Supreme Court nominees are so much less forthcoming, and that the hearings have become "vapid and hollow" as a result (Kagan 1995)? In this chapter, we identify three interrelated factors that we believe have contributed to this common—and potentially problematic—misapprehension.

The first of these factors is that critics tend to romanticize the earlier hearings, assuming that there was a "golden age" of substance and candor that no longer exists. In large part, we believe, this is a function of television—or more precisely the fact that the hearings were not televised until the 1980s. Simply put, our belief is that if the hearings had always been televised, it would be much more widely acknowledged that nominees had never been completely forthcoming, and that restraint and reticence was not, in fact, a troubling new development. Thus we think that a large part of the perception that recent nominees are so much worse than their predecessors flows from the fact that critics have simply never had the chance to watch the earlier hearings. More broadly speaking, our view is that nominees before the 1980s have gotten something of a free pass by scholars and pundits, while those since the 1980s have been much more carefully scrutinized.

A second factor that we think has given recent hearings a bad reputation falls more squarely on the nominees themselves. More specifically, our research shows that when they fail to answer Committee questions, recent nominees increasingly rely on two explanations or excuses for their lack of forthcomingness: either the question involves an issue that may come before the Court or they do not know the answer. Unfortunately for these nominees, these two particular excuses have apparently been perceived by critics as evasive tactics rather than genuine explanations.

The final piece of this misperception puzzle involves the public's appetite for answers from their Supreme Court nominees. As we discuss below, survey results from the past twenty years suggest that a majority of Americans want prospective justices to be forthcoming during their hearings. These results are not clear-cut: depending on the way in which the survey question is asked, public support for nominee responsiveness varies somewhat. However, we believe that a careful examination of the data supports our claim that Americans hold prospective justices to a very high standard of responsiveness, further fueling the perception that nominees are not doing enough when it comes to answering questions.

Taking all three of these factors together, our explanation for the persistently overstated "vapid and hollow" charge is as follows. First, in large part because of the lack of television coverage before the 1980s, critics tend to overestimate the substance and candor level of earlier hearings, which makes recent proceedings look worse by comparison. Second, the kinds of excuses that recent nominees increasingly use have apparently been interpreted as being particularly evasive. And third, the public appetite for nominee responsiveness is quite healthy, suggesting that most Americans hold prospective justices to a very high standard for candor. We turn now to each of these three factors in depth.

Television Coverage and Increasing Scrutiny of Recent Nominees

As we have discussed at length throughout this book, most critiques of Supreme Court confirmation hearings can be summed up this way: Things have really gone downhill since the 1980s. Either explicitly or implicitly, critics generally agree that the hearings have *become* less substantive, and that nominees have *become* less forthcoming, over the past few decades. That is the essence of the criticism—that things were once better than they are now. Sometimes the blame for this downward spiral is hung on Robert Bork, whose candid testimony ostensibly taught subsequent nominees that the road to confirmation was paved with evasive answers (Eisgruber 2007). Just as often, however, critics do not identify a specific turning point. They simply contend that recent nominees are worse at answering questions than earlier nominees—that they now "refus[e] to say anything meaningful" (Eisgruber 2007, 4)—and that recent hearings are worse than earlier hearings as a result.

As we now know, however, this widely shared view does not stand up to empirical testing. Nominees since the 1980s have not been markedly less forthcoming than those who came before them, and in some cases recent nominees have actually been even more willing to answer questions than their earlier counterparts. This was the core of what we showed in chapter 4.

But if this is indeed true—that is, if the pre-1980s nominees were really not that much more forthcoming than the post-1980s nominees—then why do critics consistently frame the recent hearings in such a negative light? One answer, we believe, is that because the proceedings were not televised until the 1980s, critics have focused almost all of their attention on hearings that they have seen—that is, those in the past few decades—while simply *assuming* that the earlier hearings were more substantive. Compounding this phenomenon, there has been a dramatic growth in newspaper coverage of the congressional hearings on Supreme Court nominees since the 1980s, as well as a major increase in interest group participation. Taken together, these developments have put nominees since the 1980s under a powerful microscope, while their earlier counterparts have largely escaped scrutiny. This has led critics to assume that there was a sort of "golden age" of hearings, and that the hearings they are seeing today do not measure up.

To help drive this point home, we offer data on the increase in media coverage and interest group participation, beginning with what we think may be the single-most important factor fueling the misperception about recent hearings: television.

Television

Although attempts had been made to broadcast the confirmation hearings as early as the 1960s, longtime Judiciary Committee chair James Eastland "refused to allow cameras in his committee room" (Molotsky and Weaver 1986, A10). Thus it was not until the nomination of Sandra Day O'Connor in September 1981 that the television era of Supreme Court confirmation hearings began. Part of this change can likely be attributed to the historic nature of O'Connor's nomination: she was, of course, the first woman to be formally considered for a seat on the Court. Thus, when KAET-TV, a public television station from O'Connor's home state of Arizona, requested permission to broadcast the proceedings, the Senate agreed ("O'Connor to be First Horizon Guest" 2010). The hearings were broadcast live on several PBS affiliates across the country, and were replayed in their entirety each evening on C-SPAN, the two-year-old public affairs cable network. This same coverage setup—live on PBS and a full rebroadcast on C-SPAN each evening—was in place for both William Rehnquist's and Antonin Scalia's hearings five years later, in 1986. Interestingly, C-SPAN was also able to show portions of the hearings live, but only when the House of Representatives was not in session, per C-SPAN's arrangement with Congress (Molotsky and Weaver 1986, A10; Carmody 1986, D8).

This introduction of televised coverage was a "game changer" in terms of public exposure to the confirmation hearings for two reasons. First, it allowed a mass audience to watch the proceedings either live or on rebroadcast in their entirety—something that had been impossible prior to the 1980s. But the coverage also made it much easier for Americans to watch clips of the hearings on evening news shows. Thus, between the PBS and C-SPAN coverage, on the one hand, and evening news coverage, on the other, millions of people who had never before seen a Supreme Court nominee in action were now able to do so.[1] The probable effect of this change is difficult to overstate.

Moreover, the effects grew as time went on. Coverage expanded considerably for the Robert Bork hearings in 1987, with CNN joining PBS for full live coverage, and the traditional broadcast networks, CBS, NBC, and ABC, also providing live coverage as of 2:00 p.m. each day ("TV Programs" 1987a). C-SPAN once again offered a full gavel-to-gavel rebroadcast each evening, and live coverage when the House was not in session. A similar arrangement prevailed for Anthony Kennedy's hearings in 1988 and David Souter's nomination in 1990: CNN and PBS carried the proceedings live, C-SPAN aired a full rebroadcast at night, but the traditional broadcast networks did not offer live coverage unless events warranted ("TV Programs" 1987b; "TV Programs" 1990).

For Clarence Thomas's September 1991 hearings, the viewing options expanded once again, with newly formed CourtTV and C-SPAN joining PBS and CNN with live gavel-to-gavel coverage. Interestingly, when the hearings reconvened in October after the Anita Hill allegations surfaced, CBS, NBC, and ABC joined the cable networks in providing full gavel-to-gavel coverage each day ("Television Coverage" 1991). Thus, for those hearing sessions, no fewer than seven channels were broadcasting the proceedings live—making it possible to reach a vast national audience of cable subscribers and nonsubscribers. Nielsen figures confirm that viewership was indeed substantial. During the tension-filled session on October 11, for example, Nielsen reported that nearly 30 percent of the country was tuned in, with the traditional broadcast networks generating ratings nearly twice as high as normal (Hill 1991). Meanwhile, public television stations in New York and Los Angeles recorded some of their highest ratings ever (Hill 1991). Likely anticipating a less dramatic set of events, the traditional broadcast networks pulled out of covering the next two hearings, for Ruth Bader Ginsburg in 1993 and Stephen Breyer in 1994. However, full, live coverage was still available on PBS, and CNN offered extensive live coverage as well. Meanwhile, C-SPAN continued to offer gavel-to-gavel rebroadcasts in the evening ("Hearings on Television" 1993; "Television Coverage" 1994).

By the time of John Roberts's hearings in 2005, of course, the media landscape had changed dramatically, offering new coverage options that had not existed a decade earlier. Most notably, two new 24-hour news networks, Fox News Channel and MSNBC, had been launched in the intervening years, as had C-SPAN3, creating at least three new outlets where the hearings could be broadcast live. Thus for the four most recent hearings—Roberts in 2005, Samuel Alito in 2006, Sonia Sotomayor in 2009, and Elena Kagan in 2010—the lineup has been basically the same: PBS and C-SPAN offering full live coverage, with Fox News, MSNBC, and CNN providing extensive, but not full gavel-to-gavel, live coverage. In addition to these televised options, viewers can now watch streaming coverage of the hearings at any number of websites.

As just one indication of how much the audience has grown since the days before the O'Connor hearings, Nielsen ratings data from July 14, 2009, the second day of Sotomayor's hearings were as follows: Fox News Channel had 1,083,000 viewers, CNN had 576,000 viewers, and MSNBC had 450,000 viewers. Moreover, between 5:00 p.m. and 5:45 p.m., a period when CNN stayed with the hearings with limited interruptions, it had 779,000 viewers (Cable News Ratings 2009). Again, these numbers may seem modest when compared with, say, a major sporting event, or even with the Thomas hearings, which we discussed earlier. But compared with the number of viewers that hearings before the 1980s received—essentially zero—the audience is massive. Add to that the number of Americans watching clips of the hearings on news shows and the Internet, and it is clear that Comiskey (2004, 50) is right to declare that "[t]he confirmation process is undeniably more visible since confirmation hearings were first televised in 1981."

Although televised coverage has dramatically increased the number of people who have been able to watch the proceedings, it has not come without some controversy. Carter (1994, 17), for example, contends that the coverage has "transformed an inside-the-Beltway ritual into a full-blown national extravaganza," suggesting that the hearings have become something of a media spectacle rather than a sober and substantive dialogue about constitutional issues. Another set of critics argues that the presence of cameras has led both nominees and senators to "use televised hearings as a forum," again implying that the focus is on getting a message out to the public, rather than having a substantive discussion (O'Brien 1988, 9; but see also Comiskey 2004; Watson and Stookey 1995).

As we discuss later in this chapter, we take a very different point of view on the effects of television on the hearings. But first we want to continue to build our case that increased scrutiny of the proceedings in recent decades has helped fuel the misperception that substance and candor have declined dramatically in the past few decades. To that end, we turn next to another place where coverage of the hearings has grown considerably since the 1980s: newspapers.

Newspapers

To determine whether newspaper coverage of confirmation hearings has increased in recent years, we gathered and counted the number of articles that appeared in the *New York Times* for each nominee. For each nominee we focused on the time window starting with the day of nomination by the president and extending through two days after the Senate confirmation vote (or final resolution in other cases). For the nominees from Harlan through Alito, we used the *New York Times* Historical Edition database, while for Sotomayor and Kagan we used the current database because the Historical Edition was not yet available for those recent nominees. To be included in the count, an article had to pertain to the nominee or some aspect of the confirmation hearings themselves, with at least one full paragraph devoted to the subject.[2]

Figure 6.1 plots the results of the search. We find that over time there has been an increase in the number of newspaper articles covering Supreme Court nominees. The four most recent nominees, for example, all received considerably more coverage than the first four. Some nominees in the intervening years had especially high amounts of coverage: Fortas, Haynsworth, Carswell, Bork, and Thomas. However, as we discussed in chapter 2, each of these nominations was plagued by either scandal or intense controversy. Thus the overall trend from Harlan to Kagan is a steady and significant increase in newspaper coverage.

One potential problem with the simple trend depicted in figure 6.1 is that some nominees had substantially longer confirmation time periods. As we demonstrated earlier, senators are now "slowing down the process" by extending the amount of time between the nomination and the first hearing. Therefore it is entirely possible that the increase in the number of news stories observed in figure 6.1 is wholly attributable to the fact that the news media now has substantially more time to write stories on the confirmation hearings. Therefore, we checked the robustness of this result. To do so, we standardized these story counts by the total number of days during the confirmation period, thus examining the number of articles per day. We found that the same basic trend still appears.

To be sure, this was a very simple test. However, we note that using the *Times* as a "measuring stick" is conventional practice in political science research. For example, Epstein and Segal (2000) use coverage in the *Times* (whether a story about a Court case appears on the front page or not) to determine how politically salient a Supreme Court case is to the public. And use of the *Times*

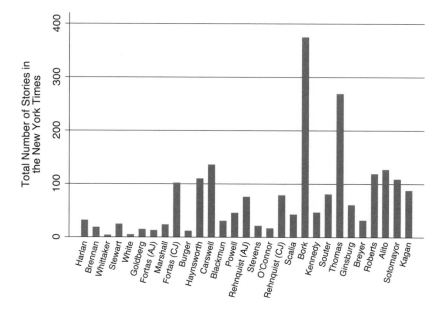

Fig. 6.1. Increasing coverage from the *New York Times*. (*Note:* See text for definition of a story. The time period extends from the day the nominee was announced through two days after the Senate vote. A similar pattern emerges when controlling for the differential length of this time period.)

is standard in other fields as well, such as tracking changes in how the media frame certain issues such as the death penalty (e.g., Baumgartner, DeBoef, and Boydstun 2008) and tracking changes in public policy agendas (e.g., Baumgartner and Jones 2009). Although critics of the *Times* may accuse it of carrying a liberal bias, there is no reason to expect that surveying the coverage of a more conservative news outlet, such as the *Wall Street Journal*, would return a different trend. In fact, we would expect to see differences only if we were to code for the positive or negative tone of the coverage, something that is beyond the scope of the project at hand.

Interest Groups

Televised broadcasts and increased newspaper coverage are not solely responsible for the disproportionate amount of scrutiny given to recent hearings, however. Another factor that has contributed to this phenomenon is the dramatic growth in interest group involvement in the confirmation process. Others have observed this phenomenon before us (see, e.g., Maltese 1995; Bell 2002; and, more recently, Stone 2011), but here we offer some new data that both updates and bolsters this well-known story.

Before turning to the data itself, we pause simply to note that Maltese's argument in particular parallels our argument here about the myth of a "golden age" of confirmation hearings. Specifically, he documents how partisan politics were present from the very beginning, starting in 1795 with the nomination of John Rutledge. His research also shows how interest groups were involved in the process early on. For example, they were involved in the successful 1881 nomination of Stanley Matthews to the Court.

With respect to the data showing the extent of interest group participation, figure 6.2 uses interest group data from Epstein et al. (2010) to graph the total number of interest groups that gave either written or oral testimony at a confirmation hearing. It is a stacked bar graph, where the number of groups opposing a nominee is stacked on top of the number of groups that supported a nominee. Thus, the absolute height of the bar represents the total participation of interest groups while the proportion of the bar is equivalent to the type of favorable or unfavorable support the nominee received. What is illuminated by figure 6.2 is that the "stacked" nature of the graph allows for a quick, visual interpretation that is intuitive. To help facilitate a proper interpretation of figure 6.2, outlier nominees, those who received an exceptionally high amount of interest group participation, were removed from the graph and are shown in figure 6.3 (more on this below).

The main finding in figure 6.2 shows that total interest group participation at the hearings has increased substantially over the last 50-plus years. Additionally, we see that during the first ten confirmation hearings, it was unusual to have more than a handful of groups give either oral or written testimony. Haynsworth's hearing was the first time that a nominee had more than ten groups participate, most of whom opposed his confirmation. This is consistent with Maltese's (1995) finding that Haynsworth's hearing was one of the earliest examples of interest groups "flexing their muscle" and influencing the confirmation process.

Starting with the nominees of the late 1960s and early 1970s, we see a small increase in the number of groups participating in the confirmation process. Additionally, figure 6.2 portrays a noteworthy trend. Although Rehnquist is the

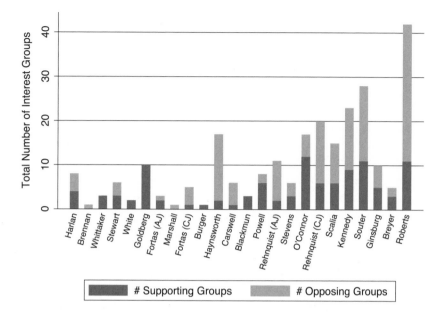

Fig. 6.2. The increasing activity of interest groups, without outliers. (Data from Epstein, Walker, Staudt, Hendrickson, and Roberts 2010. *Note:* Bork, Thomas, Alito, and Sotomayor are not shown due to exceptionally high numbers. Thornberry not shown due to lack of data.)

only other nominee in the 1970s to garner interest from more than ten interest groups, most nominees starting with O'Connor received formal attention from 15 or more interest groups (the two exceptions, Ginsburg and Breyer, received relatively low levels of attention). Nevertheless, the sharp contrast is unmistakable. What is more interesting is that we still see that a large segment of the appearing groups are there to oppose the nominees. Keep in mind that while these increases may not initially appear to be overwhelming, the figure does not include recent nominees who received an extraordinarily high level of interest group participation. Those nominees—Bork, Thomas, Alito, and Sotomayor— were not included in figure 6.2 because doing so would have distorted the figure and "masked" signs of a difference between the television and the pretelevision eras. To show how extraordinary their confirmation hearings were from the perspective of interest groups, we examine their group participation in figure 6.3.

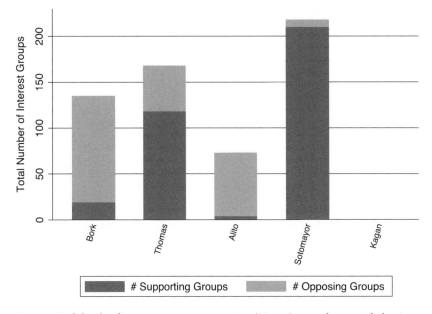

Fig. 6.3. High levels of interest group participation. (*Note:* Groups that provided written or oral testimony [data from Epstein et al. 2010]. Kagan's official data is not yet available.)

Figure 6.3 is the same type of graph—a stacked bar chart—that shows the overall level of group participation, disaggregated into supporting and opposing groups. What is striking about figure 6.3 is that all of the nominees have participation levels of well over 50 groups that either gave written or oral testimony. This is especially noteworthy because it does not include the number of groups who only participated informally in the process by externally campaigning for or against one of these nominees. Another striking feature is that two of the nominees, Thomas and Sotomayor, had very high proportions of groups supporting them, something that was enjoyed by only a few others such as O'Connor, Powell, and Goldberg.

To bolster an earlier claim, we return to examine the average level of interest group attention during the television and pretelevision eras in figure 6.4. To be sure, the figure is a simplification and we have to exercise caution when interpreting this figure because the outliers will "stretch" the averages upward, but this is to be expected and the result is nonetheless informative. For example, thinking back to figures 6.2 and 6.3, Roberts, Alito, and Sotomayor all had over

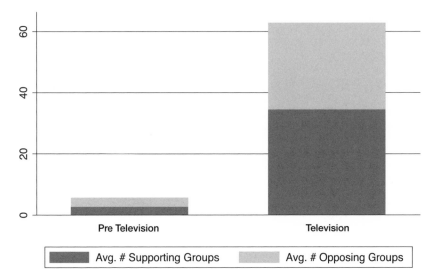

Fig. 6.4. Average interest group attention, pretelevision and television eras. (*Note:* Kagan not included in television era estimates.)

40 interest groups submit testimony. Regardless, the contrast illustrated in figure 6.3 is striking. Senators are now receiving information about the nominees from numerous groups in the form of oral or written testimony. Although we have not analyzed the content of this testimony or the formal groups submitting it, we believe it is a fairly safe assumption that both the diversity of information and groups have increased substantially. Perhaps what is more surprising, however, is that the balance between supporting and opposing groups, in the aggregate, is almost equal for both eras. Whereas the previous figures showed that some individual nominees have tended to attract either large segments of supporters or opponents, over time these groups' participation tends to balance out. In short, it is clear that interest group participation is on the rise and now appears to be a distinctive feature of our modern confirmation process.

Effects of Increased Scrutiny

Taken together, we think that these forms of increased attention (media and interest group participation) have played a pivotal role in fueling the common misperception that today's hearings are vapid and hollow in a way that earlier proceedings were not. Simply stated, because those earlier hearings largely escaped public view, there is misplaced nostalgia for a deeply substantive confirmation process that, it turns out, never really existed.

We wish to emphasize that this analysis is not in any way an indictment of those who have criticized confirmation hearings. The lack of televised coverage of the earlier hearings—the primary factor in creating this widespread misperception—is not something critics could control. As such, the tendency to talk about the older hearings as though they were part of a Golden Age of Candor is perfectly understandable given the circumstances. Our point is simply that if the earlier hearings had been as carefully scrutinized as those since the 1980s, the conventional wisdom would likely look very different, as critics would undoubtedly see that nominees have always exhibited a degree of caution—some might call it evasion—in answering questions. This might make older nominees look worse, or recent ones look better. But either way, we think that the *difference* between how the two groups answered questions is not nearly as dramatic as it is often perceived to be.

Changes in Excuses

The fact that the post-O'Connor hearings have developed a reputation for being vapid is not entirely a product of increased media attention and interest group participation, however. Some of the responsibility for this widespread perception falls on the shoulders of the nominees themselves. Clearly if every nominee since the 1980s had been answering every question in a completely forthcoming and satisfying way, there would be no way for critics to argue that the hearings lacked substance. Thus the failure or refusal of recent nominees to answer some questions has helped fuel the perception that the hearings are not substantive.[3]

But compounding this problem even further are the particular kinds of explanations or excuses that nominees offer when they do not answer questions in a fully forthcoming manner. Specifically, our research shows that nominees have relied on two particular excuses more and more over time. And as we discuss below, critics have apparently seen these two excuses as being particularly evasive.

Coding and Examples

Before turning to those findings, we offer a brief reminder of our coding scheme as it pertains to nominee excuses and explanations for not answering questions. Specifically, when we coded the hearing transcripts, we categorized nominee responses in a few different ways. First, we assessed the degree to which the nominee answered the question—forthcoming, partially forthcoming, or not forthcoming. Then, for responses that were not forthcoming (i.e., either partially forthcoming or not forthcoming at all), we looked to see if the nominee offered a reason for why he or she did not answer the question more completely. Fortunately for us, they usually did. We then placed those reasons (or what we sometimes refer to as an explanation or an excuse in this chapter) into one of six categories, which we summarize here. Below each category is an example from a transcript that we feel captures our approach to that specific coding choice.[4] Again, bear in mind that some of these were partial responses while others were not forthcoming at all. The key here is the excuse or explanation used.

(1) The issue is before the Court or could be before the Court.

> WILLIAM JENNER: I would like to know Mr. Justice Brennan's answer to that. Do you draw a distinction between international communism and communism?
>
> BRENNAN: Let me put it this way, Senator. This is the difficulty. There are cases where, as I recall it, the particular issue is whether membership, what is membership, and whether if there is membership, does that come within the purview of the congressional statutes aimed at conspiracy? I can't necessarily comment on those aspects because they are actual issues before the Court under the congressional legislation. (Brennan 1957, 20)

(2) The issue should be handled by another branch of government.

> EDWARD KENNEDY: Without in any way trying to ask you to prejudge any question or attempt to make any kind of decision, I would be interested, to the extent that you feel comfortable, in hearing from you what you consider to be perhaps the four or five most pressing questions and issues which are before the country today.

CARSWELL: That is a very difficult question, Senator. My experience, of course, has been that of a professional man in the law, as a judge primarily. I have not been in the forum or the fulcrum of the events of the day. I would certainly think that any man who was to have any exercise of power in the Supreme Court of the United States should certainly be aware of the great problems that face our country. If the past is history and the present is prologue, to that extent, certainly one must know that we have great issues in this country and many problems, as I would safely characterize them here, but I don't think it is appropriate for me to be speaking on issues per se. These would be matters more properly within the Congress in the United States to hammer out in legislation. (Carswell 1970, 24)

(3) Generalized concerns about judicial independence or prejudice.

DENNIS DECONCINI: Now, Judge Scalia, in another article in a Regulation magazine, 1982, entitled, "Freedom of Information Act Has No Clothes," you argued that the defects of the Freedom of Information Act cannot be cured as long as we are dominated by the obsession that gave them birth. You defined this obsession as the belief that the first line of defense against an arbitrary Executive is a do-it-yourself oversight by the public and its surrogates, the press. Now do you continue to believe that the Freedom of Information Act goes too far, or am I misinterpreting that article, or that paragraph I read to you?

SCALIA: Yes, I have tried to avoid making any public statements on controversial issues of public and political policy since I have been a judge, and I think I should adhere to it. What I wrote in that article is in print, and I guess you can hold it to me as being my views at that time. (Scalia 1986, 59)

(4) Not enough information to give more than a partially substantive response.

WILLIAM COHEN: One of the suggestions that has been made is that perhaps if defendants had competent counsel in the first instance, then there would be fewer reasons to have these habeas corpus petitions. I frankly take issue with that. I think a person could have the best counsel possible, and whenever someone is convicted, the first thing they are going to do is file a petition for habeas corpus, alleging incompetent counsel. That was my experience when I was practicing law, and I think it will be the experience from now into the future.

But do you have any views about whether having a cadre of professional litigants, defense counsel, would do anything to reduce the flow of petitions for habeas corpus in capital cases?

BREYER: I really don't, because of my lack of experience in that area. I think that you correctly identified what I think are the two basic considerations. (Breyer 1994, 237)

(5) Not enough information to give any substantive response.

GORDON HUMPHREY: But even during gestation, an unborn child may have an interest in an estate, may be left an estate, a legacy—is that not correct—even during gestation, and that interest can be protected under the law?

SOUTER: With respect, that is an issue which is capable of varying from jurisdiction to jurisdiction, and I will be candid to say to you that I don't recall a specific decision on it in the law of New Hampshire, which is the jurisdiction I would be familiar with. (Souter 1990, 272)

(6) Other reason or reason unclear.

BIDEN: I am not suggesting whether you are alone or in the majority. I am just trying to find out where you are. As I hear you, you do not believe that there is a general right of privacy that is in the Constitution.

BORK: Not one derived in that fashion. There may be other arguments and I do not want to pass upon those. (Bork 1987, 117)

Changes in Excuses over Time

Which of these reasons or excuses come up the most? As illustrated by figure 6.5, three excuses from the list above—number 1 (what we can call the "Live Issue" explanation), and numbers 4 and 5 (the "Don't Know" explanations)— have dominated the hearings from Harlan through Kagan. A few other features from figure 6.5 stand out as well. First, the excuses fluctuated considerably from

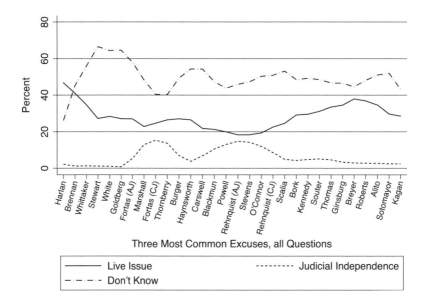

Fig. 6.5. The evolution of excuses. (*Note:* To better highlight the trends, all lines are "smoothed" using an averaging process.)

nominee to nominee. But some of the early hearings that had relatively few questions are somewhat misleading (e.g., Whittaker and White), thus making it hard to place some of those early hearings in proper perspective given that they differ in such fundamentally important ways. Second, the Live Issue excuse was declining for much of the 1960s and 1970s and reached a low mark with Stevens's hearing in 1975. However, since then that excuse has steadily become more pervasive. In fact, while this trend is often attributed to Ginsburg, it started long before Ginsburg and appears to start increasing with O'Connor. This is something we will return to more below.

Third, the Don't Know excuse might raise the issue of whether we are putting competent candidates on the bench. Is it acceptable to place a person at the highest position in our judicial system who apparently does not know answers to a number of legal and constitutional questions? Rest assured, Epstein et al. (2005) find that qualifications still play an integral role in the confirmation process. Specifically, Epstein et al. find that a nominee's lack of qualifications is a significant predictor of a senator voting against a nominee, even after controlling for ideology. Thus we suspect that if a nominee were really to exhibit widespread deficiencies in their knowledge, he or she would find considerable resistance at the committee stage.

Finally, we feel it is important to acknowledge a point about Bork's hearings that does stand out. Specifically, Bork was very reluctant to use the Live Issue excuse compared to surrounding nominees. Note that because the trend lines in figure 6.5 are averaged, the Live Issue line masks the fact that Bork used this excuse less than 10 percent of the time, far lower than any of his contemporaries. This does lend some indirect support to the argument that perhaps Bork spoke too candidly on cases that were in the "pipeline" and was punished for it (Bork 1990).

Civil Liberties

These trends are even more pronounced when we look only at questions involving civil liberties and civil rights issues. This is an important component of our investigation because civil liberties questions have become an increasingly prevalent and closely watched part of the hearings. Thus when nominees decline to answer, these excuses stand out even more. And, as we noted earlier, civil liberties questions are one place where forthcomingness has definitely dropped since Bork. Figure 6.6 contains these results, where the trend lines are "smoothed" to better depict the trends over time.

As figure 6.6 demonstrates, the Live Issue and Don't Know excuses have clearly trended upward in recent decades when those kinds of questions are asked. What this means is that while the overall level of excuses depicted in figure 6.5 has not changed dramatically, the rate at which excuses for civil rights and liberties questions are being offered has changed. As such, it seems reasonable to assume that citizens and senators alike are noticing this subtle change in trends when the questions are on a centrally important topic. Thus nominees are not only being asked more questions on these topics but they are also giving answers that are perceived to be more evasive more often. This compounds the perception of evasiveness.

Explaining the Explanations

We think that the increased use of the Live Issue and Don't Know excuses is a significant finding, as it has apparently helped fuel the perception that today's

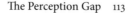

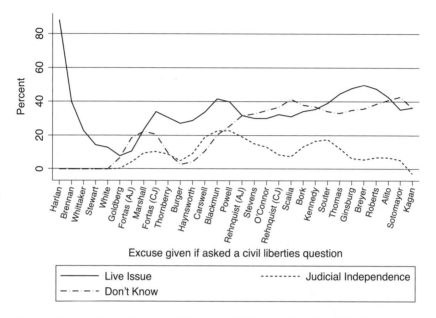

Fig. 6.6. Excuses to questions pertaining to civil rights and liberties. (*Note:* To better highlight the trends, all lines are "smoothed" using an averaging process.)

nominees are more evasive. With respect to the Don't Know excuse, the reason for this should be fairly obvious. Supreme Court nominees are generally some of the most astute legal minds in the world. Therefore, when they claim not to know how to answer a substantive legal question, it easy to see why critics might perceive this as being evasive. Similarly, the Live Issue excuse has been used so much in recent hearings that it is likely wearing thin in the eyes of critics. Certain fairly high-profile examples of this probably have not helped matters much, such as when Antonin Scalia suggested during his hearing that even *Marbury v. Madison*, the landmark 1803 case establishing judicial review, was somewhat off limits because it was a "specific Supreme Court opinion" (Scalia 1986, 33). Here again, it is easy to see why critics have bristled at this sort of excuse, which has been on the rise in recent years.

The Live Issue explanation is particularly interesting because, from the nominee's point of view, it is likely seen as a legitimate claim, not an evasive tactic. For one thing, all judges are expected to subscribe to the same canon of ethics, whether they are a sitting judge on another court, or a judge that may be sitting on the Supreme Court in the near future. For example, Canon 2 of the American Bar Association Model Code of Judicial Conduct states that any judicial candidate should disqualify himself or herself from any case in which he or she has made a "public statement" that "appears to commit" the judge to a particular result.[5]

Moreover, nominees in recent years have actually been advised to offer this explanation as a way to avoid the appearance of prejudice. For example, Rutkus (2005) reports that in the time period leading up to O'Connor's confirmation hearings, John Roberts, who at the time was special assistant to the attorney general, wrote a memorandum refuting the argument that nominees could openly answer questions about cases, even if there was an understanding that "no promises" were made, because there would still be the appearance of impropriety.[6] Figure 6.7 shows the memo.[7] This memo seems to help explain why the Live Issue excuse has been on the rise since O'Connor's hearing. Unfortunately, if critical responses to the hearings are any indicator, it appears that nominees have begun to use it too much.

Bringing the Public In

Thus far we have identified two factors that have fueled the perception that recent hearings are more vapid and hollow than earlier ones. We now turn to what we believe is a third factor: public opinion—or, more specifically, the public's desire to get answers from Supreme Court nominees.

Public Opinion and Confirmation Hearings

That there is a two-way connection between public opinion and Supreme Court confirmation hearings has been established by previous research. For example, with regard to the effect of the hearings on public attitudes toward the nominees, Caldeira and Smith (1996) examined four waves of public opinion data during the Thomas hearings to identify shifts in support. They showed that when the hearings began, blacks were only slightly more positive than whites toward the Thomas nomination. However, when the Anita Hill allegations surfaced, and Thomas famously rebuked the Committee for engaging in a "high-tech lynching" (Thomas 1991, pt. 4, 157), public support among blacks increased to a point where most black liberals no longer opposed his nomination (Caldeira and Smith 1996).

Office of the Attorney General
Washington, D. C. 20530
September 9, 1981

TO   :   Sandra Day O'Connor

FROM   :   John Roberts *John Roberts*
              Special Assistant to the Attorney General

SUBJECT   :   Rees Memorandum

     The attached memorandum from Professor Rees to the Subcommittee on Separation of Powers on the proper scope of questioning Supreme Court nominees does not require any modification of the views expressed in your August 28 letter to Senator Helms. Professor Rees argues that the only practical manner in which Senators can discharge their responsibility to ascertain the views of a nominee is to ask specific questions on actual (though nonpending) or hypothetical cases. He stresses that questions on general judicial philosophy are too indeterminate and notes that nominees have often decided cases in a manner inconsistent with the views they expressed on judicial philosophy at their confirmation hearings.

     Professor Rees argues that if a nominee stated her views on a specific question it would not be grounds for later disqualification. He relies on Justice Rehnquist's opinion in Laird v. Tatum, dismissing Justice Rehnquist's distinction between statements prior to nomination and those after nomination. According to Rees, statements after nomination would not be disqualifying if the nominee and Senators understood that no promises on future votes were intended. Professor Rees concludes by citing past confirmation hearing practice which he contends supports his view.

     The proposition that the only way Senators can ascertain a nominee's views is through questions on specific cases should be rejected. If nominees will lie concerning their philosophy they will lie in response to specific questions as well. The suggestion that a simple understanding that no promise is intended when a nominee answers a specific question will completely remove the disqualification problem is absurd. The appearance of impropriety remains. Professor Rees' citations to past practice do reveal some possible indiscretions, but the generally established practice is as indicated in your letter to Senator Helms, which contains supporting citations.

Fig. 6.7. Memo from John Roberts to Sandra Day O'Connor. (Image from National Archives: http://www.archives.gov/news/john-roberts/accession-60-88-0498/026-ocon nor-misc/folder026.pdf.)

Research exploring the other direction—the influence of public opinion on the hearings—shows that constituent preferences can affect how senators vote on nominees. For example, Overby et al. (1992, 1994) found that the percentage of African Americans in a state influenced the likelihood of voting "yes" on the Thomas and Marshall confirmations. Unfortunately, these studies relied primarily on state-level data without any connection to constituent preferences (but see Overby and Brown [1997] who incorporate exit poll data to measure characteristics of reelection constituencies). Recently, however, Kastellec, Lax, and Phillips (2010) have provided a more direct assessment. Specifically, they examined several national polls over the last ten nominees and, utilizing a range of statistical and methodological advancements, were able to provide a link between individual citizen preferences and a senator's votes—a link that holds even after controlling for other likely explanations of the senator's voting behavior. In short, the public does have an opinion on Supreme Court nominees and senators are aware of it when voting on their confirmation.

The Public's Desire to Know

Clearly, as coverage of the hearings has increased over the past three decades, the public's awareness of the confirmation process has grown. At the same time, the chorus of criticism of the hearings and the nominees has been increasingly difficult to ignore. Based on these developments, it seems fair to assume that citizens would have strong opinions about the confirmation process regarding their expectations that Supreme Court nominees answer questions in a forthcoming manner. In particular, we think it likely that Americans will not be tolerant of nominees who do not respond fully to questions during their hearings.

To examine public opinion on nominee candor, we compare the results of several national survey questions taken over a span of nearly twenty years—starting in 1991 and ranging through 2010—that gauged public attitudes toward nominee candor. Regrettably (from the point of view of consistency at least) the questions across surveys are not identical.[8] However, we believe that when all of the poll results are considered together, the findings help explain the misperception puzzle that we are trying to solve. Moreover, a closer look at the question variation actually sheds light on some of the complexities of public attitudes toward Supreme Court nominee responsiveness.

Table 6.1 displays the weighted results of seven questions that ask some variation of the same question. The nominees include Thomas, Roberts, and

Kagan.[9] The questions all ask whether the respondent thinks the nominee should have to state his or her views. Although some questions ask about "issues" in general, others ask about past cases or about abortion specifically, a perennially "hot" topic (see Ringhand and Collins 2011).[10] Every question in table 6.1 shows majority support for having nominees answer questions (or that it is not acceptable for nominees to decline to answer them). Moreover, five out of the seven questions show over 60 percent support for the idea that the nominee should answer questions. Thus, the pattern is unmistakable. In addition, we should note that very few people expressed "don't know" or had no opinion on the topic. In sum, based on these results, it appears that the public has had a strong appetite for having nominees answer questions over at least the past twenty years.

One important potential caveat here is that all seven questions ask respondents to consider nominee forthcomingness in a very straightforward, one-dimensional manner. That is, none of these questions hint that there may be another side to the issue. By contrast, if survey respondents were told that nominees had a legitimate excuse for not answering questions—for example, the issue might appear before the Court in the future—might this change things? That is, if citizens were to consider nominee forthcomingness from more than one point of view, and not just from the perspective of simple candor, what would public opinion look like?

Table 6.2 displays the results to three questions we found where the question wording suggested that there may be a legitimate reason for nominees not to answer the question. The first question for Clarence Thomas suggests that he might have to rule on those future cases that he is asked about; the second question raises the notion of partisan fairness by suggesting that Roberts might not have to answer questions because Ginsburg chose not to answer some questions; and the third question reminds survey respondents that past nominees have not answered questions, implying that when Roberts does not answer these questions he is not breaking any Senate norm or precedent (and in fact, he is in keeping with past norms).

The results in table 6.2 are striking, especially considering how one sided the results were in table 6.1. Indeed, the percentage of the public that believes nominees should have to answer questions ranges from a high of only 43 percent down to 20 percent. In addition, one of the questions even suggests that there may be a large portion of the public that does not have a firm attitude on the subject (16% said "don't know" or "no opinion" for Roberts on July 26–27,

TABLE 6.1. Public Opinion toward Candor

Nominee	Question Wording	Should Answer/ Not Acceptable to Decline	Should NOT have to answer/ Acceptable to Decline	Don't Know/ No Opinion	Source
Thomas	During the confirmation process before the U.S. Senate, do you think Clarence Thomas should or should not have to state his views on abortion and other important issues that may come before the Supreme Court?	60%	35%	5%	NBC News, Wall Street Journal, conducted by Hart-Teeter Research Companies. July 26–July 29, 1991. Question 14d. N = 1,004 registered voters.
Roberts	At his confirmation hearing, do you think Roberts should or should not answer questions about how he would have ruled on past cases that have come before the Supreme Court?	61%	36%	3%	ABC News/Washington Post Supreme Court Poll, July 21, 2005 (ICPSR Study #4332), Question #4. N = 500; weighted responses.
Roberts	Do you think Roberts should or should not publicly state his position on abortion before being approved by the U.S. Senate for the job?	63%	34%	3%	ABC News/Washington Post Supreme Court Poll, July 21, 2005 (ICPSR Study #4332), Question #5. N = 500; weighted responses.
Roberts	At his confirmation hearing, do you think (Supreme Court nominee John) Roberts should or should not answer questions about how he would have ruled on past cases that have come before the Supreme Court?	53%	42%	5%	ABC News/Washington Post, August 25–August 28, 2005. N = 1,006 phone interviews of national adults. Interviews were conducted by TNS Intersearch, Question #30. Weighted responses.

Roberts	Do you think Roberts should or should not publicly state his position on abortion before being approved by the U.S. Senate for the job?	61%	36%	3%	ABC News/Washington Post, August 25–August 28, 2005. N = 1,006 phone interviews of national adults. Interviews were conducted by TNS Intersearch, Question #31. Weighted responses.
Kagan	At her confirmation hearing, do you think Kagan should or should not answer questions about how she would have ruled on past cases that have come before the Supreme Court?	66%	29%	5%	ABC News/Washington Post, June Monthly Poll. June 3–June 6, 2010. Question #34, N = 498 (split sample) weighted.
Kagan	Do you think Kagan should or should not publicly state her position on abortion before being approved by the U.S. Senate for the job?	53%	42%	5%	ABC News/Washington Post, June Monthly Poll. June 3–June 6, 2010, Question #35, N = 499 (split sample) weighted.

Note: All responses are weighted based on sample survey specifications.

TABLE 6.2. Multidimensionality of Public Opinion toward Candor

Nominee	Question Wording	Should Answer/ Not Acceptable to Decline	Should NOT have to answer/ Acceptable to Decline	Don't Know/ No Opinion	Source
Thomas	At the Senate hearings Thomas has declined to discuss his views on abortion laws. He said he should not comment on matters that might become Supreme Court cases on which he would have to rule. Do you think Thomas should or should not have discussed his views on abortion laws at the hearings?	37%	61%	2%	ABC News/ Washington Post Clarence Thomas Hearing Poll, September 13–15, 1991 (ICPSR 9767, Question #22) $N = 1,233$; weighted responses.
Roberts	In her confirmation hearings for the Supreme Court, (Bill) Clinton nominee Ruth Bader Ginsburg chose not to answer certain questions about her personal views on some issues because she was concerned about commenting on issues that might come before her as a judge. John Roberts may not answer certain questions for the same reasons. Is that acceptable or not acceptable?	20%	76%	3%	New Models National Brand Poll, July 23–24, 2005, of 1,000 phone interviews of registered voters. Retrieved Feb.13, 2013, from the iPOLL Databank, The Roper Center for Public Opinion Research, University of Connecticut. http://www.ropercenter.uconn.edu/data_access/ipoll/ipoll.html.

Roberts

In previous Senate con-
firmation hearings, some
nominees have refused to
answer questions related to
past Supreme Court cases
or cases that may come
before the Court in the
future. Do you think this is
acceptable or unacceptable
for John Roberts to decline
to answer questions on past
or future cases before the
Supreme Court?

43%

41%

16%

Survey by Fox News con-
ducted by Opinion Dynam-
ics, July 26–27, 2005, based
on 990 phone interviews
with national registered
voters.

Note: All responses are weighted based on sample survey specifications.

2005)—something that was absent in table 6.1. In sum, the results of table 6.2 are almost the exact opposite of those displayed in table 6.1, and the importance behind it becomes salient when we focus on the substantive differences in question wording.

Given the extensive research on question wording effects in survey research, this is hardly surprising. It is well known, for example, that response distributions can and often do shift when the question wording changes even though the underlying meaning does not. One commonly accepted explanation for this is that citizens are merely responding to questions based on whatever consideration is at the "top of their heads" (e.g., Zaller 1992). Perhaps the classic example of a question framing experiment is by Tversky and Kahneman (1982) who show that citizens answer differently depending on question wording even though the meaning of the question is the same (e.g., by framing something in terms of a "loss" or a "gain"). More relevant to our inquiry, Sniderman and Theriault (2004) show that when citizens are exposed to two sides of the issue, rather than only one side, citizen responses will look different (and less pliable).

Ultimately, however, our view is that in this particular instance at least, the one-sided surveys are actually more telling of public attitudes on the issue of nominee candor. More precisely, our belief is that the majority of Americans have not explored the complexities of nominee candor all that much—most likely, we suspect, because confirmations are relatively infrequent and not regular events, leaving citizens little time or necessity to think about them extensively. As such, the average citizen's thoughts and understanding of the issue are probably closer to the "one-sided" poll question. Thus when we see that a strong majority of Americans say that they want nominees to answer questions, we believe this likely reflects where the public stands on the issue, unless, of course, they are forced to think about confirmation hearings with more depth. And this healthy appetite for answers, in turn, helps explain why there is such a strong perception that nominees are not doing a good enough job during their hearings.

There is one final element in why we think the "conventional wisdom" of "evasive nominees" persists in American society. This chapter has laid out evidence for our three arguments on why we think this belief persists, even with little or no evidence to support this belief. We also recognize that there is another theoretical explanation for this persistence that is entirely consistent with our explanations, though we have not tested it directly because it is beyond the scope of this book. The perception gap could partly stem from something that psychologists call "confirmation bias" (no pun intended), where the predominant social theory perseveres despite weak or absent evidence, or even contradictory evidence (Anderson, Lepper, and Ross 1980). While it is not necessary to get into the details of the explanation, we feel it is necessary to mention it because it is a complementary theory about the psychological origins of the explanations that we offered in this chapter.

Conclusion

In this chapter we sought to explain why recent Supreme Court nominees have developed a reputation for being so much more evasive than their predecessors when, in fact, things have not changed all that much over the years. Three factors have led to this misperception. First and foremost, hearings since the 1980s have been televised, covered more by the news media, and have played a more central role in American life. As a result, critics have been able to romanticize earlier proceedings—significantly "rounding up" the degree to which pre-O'Connor nominees answered questions—which has made recent hearings look less substantive by comparison. Second, when they do not answer questions, nominees have increasingly offered explanations that critics apparently perceive to be particularly evasive. And lastly, the public appetite for answers, when considered only as a one-dimension issue, has been consistently strong, which appears to fit how the issue is most often discussed. However, only when the public considers other factors affecting this issue does the public's expectations of forthcomingness drop. Together, these three factors have created a kind of "perfect storm" whereby recent nominee performances have been framed as being significantly less forthcoming and less substantive than earlier testimony, when in fact the differences are not that great.

The precise effects of this widespread misperception may be difficult to prove empirically, but we think they are potentially quite serious. For one thing, it is our firm belief that senators think that modern nominees are more evasive. Interestingly, as our research in chapter 5 illustrated, members of the Judiciary Committee do not appear to be influenced as much by this perceived lack of candor as by partisan considerations. But this does not mean that the perception of evasiveness is not affecting these senators at all. It may be influencing the kinds of questions they ask, or the way in which they ask them. For example, one need not strain to see how a perception of declining responsiveness would make senators more combative toward nominees, which in turn could affect the complexion of the confirmation process writ large. Moreover, the relentless refrain from both senators and members of the media about nominee evasiveness is sure to undermine the public's perception of nominees, who then usually become justices. Over time, this could help lead to a deterioration in public support for the justices, even if institutional legitimacy levels for the Court itself remain high (see, e.g., Caldeira and Gibson 1992; Gibson, Caldeira, and Spence 2003). Indeed, Gibson and Caldeira (2009) find that politicized confirmation battles pose a threat to the legitimacy of the Supreme Court.

Accordingly, we think that the persistent misperception that attends modern confirmation hearings is hardly just an academic concern. It is likely having an effect on how the hearings function, and how Supreme Court justices are perceived by elected officials, the press, and the public. Understanding the sources of that misperception, we hope, will at least serve as a first step toward moving past it.

We close this chapter by raising an interesting normative issue that will serve as a transition to our final chapter. As we noted throughout this book, though especially in the opening chapters, there is substantial concern over whether confirmation hearings are functioning in a manner that is satisfactorily consistent with how it is spelled out in the U.S. Constitution. Stated another way, there is a widespread perception that these confirmation hearings are broke and that senators cannot fulfill their constitutional "consent" function if nominees do not answer questions. However, we found that when the public is asked to consider the hearings in the context of competing issues (e.g., the need for answers from the nominee vs. some legitimate reasons for not answering questions), then the public does a complete 180 degree turn and supports the nominees not answering questions. Seen in this light, it appears that any concern over the functionality of the hearings lacks majority support, at least among the public. If anything, this tells us that we should be cautious about relying on just a single poll, and even more cautious about drawing any substantive conclusions about the health of the hearings that are not adequately addressed in the question wording themselves. This is important because relying on one-sided polls can create a false perception. And in a representative democracy like the United States, to the extent that senators rely on public opinion polls, this creates a major concern about how senators make decisions when weighing evidence of their constituent's preferences.

SEVEN

Can the Hearings Be Improved?
Do They Need to Be?

As criticism of Supreme Court confirmation hearings has intensified over the past few decades, so have calls for reforming the process. Some have argued that the Judiciary Committee should limit the scope of its questioning to issues of character and competence (Carter 1988; Rotunda 2001). Others have gone the other way, arguing that nominees should be expected to explain their views on legal and constitutional issues in depth (Gerhardt 1992; Kagan 1995; Post and Siegel 2006; Strauss and Sunstein 1992). Although their approaches differ, these calls for change do have at least one of two things in common. The first is that they are based on a shared assumption that the hearings are no longer working as well as they should. And the second is that they have not worked.

In this chapter, we bring our work on the confirmation hearings into this debate by looking at some of the proposals for change in more detail. We then explain why we think that they have not been effective to date, and why some of the findings that we have made in this book could help change that. Ultimately, our view is that critics have overestimated the degree to which the hearings need to be changed, while at the same time underestimating how difficult it is to change them. We offer a more modest and focused proposal, based on the central findings of this book, that we believe addresses both of these shortcomings. We close by explaining why we think the more pressing need is not in reforming the hearings, but rather in reforming how we perceive them.

Why It Matters

Before turning to these reform proposals, it is worthwhile to take a step back and ask why it is important for the confirmation hearings to work effectively in the first place. Why are critics so concerned that there is something wrong?

The most straightforward answer is accountability. One of the central principles of our constitutional system is the belief that government officials should be accountable to the public. Among elected politicians, such as the president and members of Congress, this accountability comes through the voting booth. But for the federal judiciary, there is no such direct mechanism. As such, unelected judges and justices always run the risk of being seen as illegitimate authorities in a democracy: citizens might ask at any moment why they should live under rules made by individuals who were appointed and not elected.

To mitigate some of these concerns, while still keeping the judiciary at a safe distance from day-to-day political pressures, the constitutional framers provided the Senate, in Article II, with the power to give "advice and consent" on presidential appointments, including federal judges and justices. Under this arrangement, there is a connection (albeit an indirect one) between the public and the judiciary, as elected representatives must give approval to all nominations.[1] In theory, then, confirmation hearings can help confer legitimacy on the courts by providing an element of democratic accountability to an otherwise unaccountable institution (see Ringhand and Collins 2011). And by extension, since it is Supreme Court justices who are largely responsible for interpreting and defining the Constitution, it is fair to say that the Senate's advice and consent role in judicial nominations actually "underwrites the democratic accountability of constitutional law" (Post and Siegel 2006, 39). That is, the confirmation hearings supply a crucial link between citizens, who live under the Constitution, and Supreme Court justices, who largely determine the way in which the Constitution operates and how it affects the public.

But if judicial nominees are not being sufficiently forthcoming during this critical phase in the confirmation process, where does that leave "democratic accountability"? Why should a citizen put his or her faith in Supreme Court justices who have not in fact been held accountable? Confidence and trust in unelected officials is tenuous enough on its own. But if there is no meaningful vetting process prior to the lifetime appointment of a Supreme Court justice—

one of just nine individuals empowered to rule on the most important and controversial issues affecting public life—then why should the Court be considered a legitimate decision-making authority?

The Calls for Change

Against this background, it is hardly surprising that there have been countless suggestions over the past two decades for how to fix the confirmation hearings. Though the proposals differ, they are united around the idea that there is something wrong with the way the process works now—either because senators are asking questions that they should not be asking or because nominees are not answering questions that they should be answering. Other, more radical calls for change have been offered as well, such as abolishing the "hollow spectacle" of the hearings altogether (Greenbaum 2010). But we focus here on what we think are the most realistic and reasonable suggestions—those having to do with reforming the question-and-answer component of the hearings themselves.

Roughly speaking, proposals for changing the hearings along these lines can be broken down into two groups. The first group, most closely associated with Stephen Carter's widely cited 1988 article "The Confirmation Mess," suggests that senators should not expect nominees to answer questions about their approach to specific cases or even their judicial philosophy (see also Fein 1989; Rotunda 2001). Instead, committee members should focus on the nominee's moral character. Carter's argument essentially boils down to this: focusing on specifics, rather than temperament, impedes an independent judiciary by allowing the Senate to approve only those candidates whose views align with the majority. That is, if the Court is supposed to act as a countermajoritarian check on majority excesses—if it is supposed to be the "brake" in our political system—then it is crucial for the justices not to always be part of that majority. And if the Senate only approves justices with whose views they agree, then, by definition, those justices are unlikely to be part of a countermajoritarian force. Instead, Carter argues, the committee should focus on a nominee's "moral instincts," and not policy preferences nor constitutional theory. As he famously puts it, nominees should be those "for whom moral choices occasion deep and sustained reflection" and "whose personal moral decisions seem generally sound" (Carter 1988, 1199).

The second group goes the other way, arguing that the hearings work best when nominees answer more questions, not fewer. A range of proposals falls into this category. Some suggest that nominees should be expected to answer questions about their judicial philosophy—their general approach to interpreting the Constitution—but not about specific cases. This approach seeks to preserve some of the deeper questions that senators might want to ask while simultaneously keeping nominees away from "hot button issues of the day," which tend to politicize the confirmation process and make the Court look like a political institution (Goldberg 2004, 194; see also Tribe 1985). Thus by inquiring about ideology and judicial philosophy but not specific cases, senators can "ensure that no single philosophy dominates the Court" while still allowing nominees to remain outside of the political process (Goldberg 2004, 194). So, under this framework, senators would undertake only "a *somewhat* more probing examination of Supreme Court nominees" (Ringhand 2008, 5). Critics of this approach, however, charge that that it "is not so much a compromise as it is a capitulation" (Ringhand 2007, 7), meaning that it stops short of doing what needs to be done—namely, getting nominees to reveal more about their views prior to being confirmed.

Others within this second camp envision an even more robust role for the Senate in questioning and assessing nominees. Specifics here differ, with some suggesting that nominees should be expected to answer questions about any legal issue or case (Lively 1986), and others arguing that the focus should be on previously decided cases (Post and Siegel 2006). The Post-Siegel proposal—to limit questions to cases that have already been decided—has probably attracted the most attention in recent years. As Post and Siegel see it, their approach would turn the hearings into "a colloquy capable of adequately informing a senatorial vote on whether to invest a nominee with the independent authority to interpret the Constitution" (45). That is, it would give senators enough information to make an informed decision on the nominee without simultaneously asking the nominee to violate any perceived norms regarding prejudice or bias concerning possible future cases.

Critiques of the Proposals

Both of these approaches have their fair share of detractors. For example, with regard to the proposals to limit questions to issues of character and competence, Ringhand (2009) highlights one very serious potential flaw. Specifically, she argues that Carter's theory is predicated on two false assumptions about the Court: one that it is a countermajoritarian institution, and the other that justices actually use constitutional theory (as opposed to policy preferences) to decide cases (4–5). This "conventional narrative" about the Court has been largely discredited by empirical research over the past half century (see, e.g. Dahl 1957; Marshall 1989; Segal and Spaeth 1996, 2002). Therefore, she argues, there is no reason not to ask prospective justices about their judicial philosophy or ideological views. To the contrary, if indeed justices are making decisions based on their own political preferences, and are "*not* using objective interpretive methods to find and impose fixed constitutional constraints," then it is not only acceptable but rather *essential* for senators to determine each nominee's preferences and ideology. As she argues, "surely the people and their representatives can claim some right to guide that process by ascertaining the ideological preferences of nominees before confirming them to a lifetime position on the high court" (Ringhand 2009, 137). The notion that senators should stay away from substantive legal and constitutional questions only makes sense if one believes that justices are actually making decisions entirely based on objective constitutional theories that allow them to remain independent from the political sphere. Otherwise, those things should be fair game.

Another serious problem with the Carter approach is that it signals a retreat for those interested in getting *more* answers from Supreme Court nominees. Carter was writing, of course, in the immediate aftermath of the Bork hearings, and it is not hard to see the influence of that episode in his proposal. Rather than putting nominees through another Bork-like inquisition, which might threaten the independence of the judiciary, he believed that the Senate should go the other way and focus on issues of character and competence. But what one gains from Carter's proposal in eliminating tension and conflict, one loses in substance. Putting such a large bundle of questions off limits might increase the percentage of forthcoming answers that nominees provide, but only because the number of substantive questions had been substantially reduced. This would seem to be a Pyrrhic victory at best for reformers who seek to have more candor injected into the process.

But the other approach—the one that advocates asking nominees more questions—has its drawbacks as well. One particularly difficult idea is that nominees and senators often have different views on what is "settled" law. Thus, while it might be a good idea in theory to ask nominees about previously decided cases, in practice this becomes more difficult. We have seen this quite a bit in our own research, where nominees claim that they cannot answer questions about past cases because the issues could come up again. As we noted earlier, this can reach extremes, such as when Justice Scalia declined to opine on *Marbury v. Madison*. But more often, the distinction is subtler than that, and while senators might consider the case closed, nominees might claim that it is off limits because it could come up again in the future.

The other obvious shortcoming here is that even if senators somehow persuade nominees to answer these kinds of questions, there is no way to ensure that their responses will line up with their actions once they are confirmed. Recent work by Czarnezki, Ford, and Ringhand (2007) illustrates this problem well. Using hearing transcripts from all of the justices on the Rehnquist natural court, Czarnezki, Ford, and Ringhand coded nominee statements about various substantive constitutional questions, such as the importance of original meaning or the constitutional rights of criminal defendants. They then compared these statements to how the justices voted once on the Court. Their results show little correlation, suggesting that while nominees all tend to express similar ideas about substantive issues during their hearings, these views do not often carry over to the Court itself, where they approach and decide cases very differently. In short, even if nominees do answer more questions, it is not clear that this has much of an effect on their decision making. Short of impeaching sitting justices for deviating from their testimony—a proposal that not even the most dissatisfied critic is likely to endorse—it is not entirely clear how simply asking questions about specific legal and constitutional issues will improve the hearings on its own.

Why the Proposals Have Not Worked

The critiques outlined above certainly raise questions about whether these approaches are a good idea. But what they do not illuminate as clearly is why they have not yet worked. Using the findings we have discussed throughout this book, we can now identify at least three reasons why these calls for change may have not met with much success.

The first problem with most hearing reform proposals is that they are often predicated on the assumption that the hearings changed for the worse after the 1980s. That is, reformers generally assume that Bork's candid responses during his hearing taught subsequent nominees to duck, dodge, and evade any questions that could threaten their nomination prospects. Consider, for example, Kagan's famous charge that the hearings are "vapid and hollow." In its full context, the real message becomes clear:

> The Bork hearings presented to the public a serious discussion of the meaning of the Constitution, the role of the Court, and the views of the nominee; that discussion at once educated the public and allowed it to determine whether the nominee would move the Court in the proper direction. Subsequent hearings have presented to the public a vapid and hollow charade, in which repetition of platitudes has replaced discussion of viewpoints and personal anecdotes have supplanted legal analysis. (Kagan 1995, 941)

Note Kagan's reference to "subsequent hearings"—that is, those after Bork. So the idea here, for Kagan and for almost all critics of the hearings, is that the hearings have *become* problematic, or that they have *become* less substantive—not that they have always been that way.

But as we have shown throughout this book, and in particular in chapters 4 and 5, that is not actually the case. With respect to nominee testimony—to how often nominees answer questions in a forthcoming manner—the hearings have not changed all that much since they began in 1955. Instead, the level of responsiveness to Judiciary Committee questioning has been fairly stable, with most nominees hovering around the same levels of forthcoming responses. There have been ebbs and flows, to be sure, and as we showed in chapter 5, polarization has indirectly affected forthcomingness through partisanship and ideology in voting. But this should not overshadow the fact that some early nominees were considerably less forthcoming than some of their modern counterparts. Thus the notion that the hearings have become significantly less substantive over time—and that there was a kind of "golden age" of hearings prior to the 1980s when nominees were always more willing to answer questions—is untenable. Nominees have always declined to answer questions to some degree; it is not a recent phenomenon.

To be sure, the hearings are not the same today as they were when they began more than a half century ago. The most obvious changes involve their length and their format. Early hearings often comprised fewer than 100 questions, and took less than a day to complete. Now they are multiday affairs where nominees are asked between 500 and 700 questions. Moreover, the hearings used to be much more freewheeling affairs, where some senators would dominate the questioning while others remained silent. Today, each member of the Judiciary Committee is given time to ask questions, and they use all of it. As a result, there is much more balance between parties in terms of question-asking, and the questioning is spread out fairly evenly among committee members. Other, less obvious changes have occurred as well. Among these, we consider the most notable to be the increase in the number of questions involving civil liberties or civil rights issues. Clearly as the Court ventured further into the "storm center" of American political life (O'Brien 2011)—and in particular after its decision in *Roe v. Wade*—it became increasingly important for senators to satisfy their constituents by probing nominees for their views on hot-button issues such as abortion rights, capital punishment, affirmative action, school prayer, and same-sex marriage.

But however significant these changes might be, we think the more remarkable phenomenon is how little nominee testimony has changed against this background. And we think that this has been a blind spot for the hearing reform effort. That is, rather than focusing on the hearings as a whole, critics have assumed that the problem is that post-Bork nominees have trimmed their sails in order to avoid controversy and maximize their chances of being confirmed. But when one recognizes that nominees have always exhibited a mix of forthcomingness and evasion, of responsiveness and caution, the calculus for changing the hearings looks very different. Fixing the process is not a matter of "rewinding the tape" a few decades and restoring the dynamic that existed prior to the 1980s. Whatever one says about how Justice Sonia Sotomayor performed at her hearing, one should also say about Justice Potter Stewart. Thus before any proposed fixes can be expected to work, they should first be sure they are focused on the right defect.

A second, closely related problem with existing reform proposals is that they tend to overestimate nominee evasiveness. To hear critics tell it, most modern Supreme Court nominees say almost nothing of substance during their hearings. But when one looks at the data that we present in chapter 4, this characterization seems at least a bit exaggerated. Every nominee that we analyzed, save for Fortas during his hearing to be Chief Justice, answered at least 60 percent of the questions they were asked in a forthcoming manner, and even the most recent nominees are in the 70 percent range. By contrast, refusals to answer (our "Not Forthcoming" category) make up less than 10 percent on average. Thus for nearly every nominee, some kind of substantive answer was given to roughly nine out of every ten questions. We do not think this neatly fits the definition of "vapid and hollow."

Two important caveats apply here. First, we do not mean to suggest that the hearings—either before the 1980s or after—are beyond criticism. To the contrary, we think it is a perfectly reasonable interpretation of our data to say that some of the hearings have lacked substance. Although it is true that most nominees answered more than 60 or 70 percent of their questions in a way that could be described as fully forthcoming, this also means that three or four out of every ten questions get either a partial answer or no answer at all. We read-ily acknowledge that this could be interpreted as being problematic. Second, because of the nature of our coding method, there may be some answers that were coded as Forthcoming but that other observers would find either unsatis-fying or even inaccurate. Our primary goal was to identify responses based on how willing the nominee was to provide an answer, not the degree to which we thought it was the *best* answer the nominee could have provided. Thus it is pos-sible, or even likely, that one of the reasons that critics see the hearings as less substantive than we do is that they see places where nominees could have said more, or done a better job in answering questions. But this is a problem with the questioning by the senators, who could have asked follow-up questions if they were unhappy with the answers, rather than the quality of the answers provided by the nominees.

Nevertheless, we stand firmly by our assessment that all of the confirmation hearings from 1955 forward have been more substantive than the conventional wisdom would have us believe. And as such, we think that most proposals for changing the hearings are too sweeping, calling to mind the old adage "trying to kill a fly with an axe." It is true that nominees are not fully forthcoming all of the time. But the notion that the hearings are essentially devoid of substance has, we believe, led critics to suggest changes that may be more dramatic than they need to be. When combined with the first concern we identified above, this has created a situation where calls for change are simultaneously too nar-row, because they assume the problem is relatively new, and too broad, because they assume the problem is worse than it is. Our feeling is that these are not sound fundamentals on which to build any reform proposal.

The final "blind spot" that seems to hinder reform efforts involves the idea of incentives. Specifically, critics often propose changes that depend on nomi-nees changing how they approach their testimony. For example, the entire line of proposals calling for tougher Senate questioning assumes that at some point nominees will actually answer these questions. But the problem, of course, is that nominees have little incentive to do so. If previous nominees have been able to secure confirmation without answering every question that senators might want to ask them, then why would future nominees risk their confirmation by increasing their level of responsiveness? After all, "[t]he nominees' incentives . . . are almost always to provide as little information as possible" (Czarnezki, Ford, and Ringhand 2007, 160). In this way, we agree with those who say that calls for "cooperative" nominees (Eisgruber 2007, 173) are "unrealistic" and "not viable" (Stras and Scott 2008, 1892).

This does not mean that there is no way to improve the hearings along these lines, however. It just means that whatever change is going to occur is going to have to be because senators start punishing nominees by voting against them if they do not answer enough questions. Certainly we have seen senators in recent years saying that they would do this. For example, as we saw in chapter 5, Chuck Schumer told Samuel Alito that "the first criterion" he would use in deciding whether to vote "yes" or "no" was whether Alito was prepared to "answer questions fully and forthrightly." Likewise, from the other side of the aisle, Senator George Lemieux justified his vote against Elena Kagan's nomination this way: "If she had been more forthcoming, perhaps I would have been able to come to a different conclusion" (Derby 2010).

The problem, of course, is that, especially in recent years, senators have talked tough when it comes to the issue of nominees answering questions, but they have not often followed through. This was what we discovered in chapter 5, where the results of a multivariate test showed that nominee responsiveness played a much bigger role in determining committee votes from 1955 to 1975 than from 1975 forward. By contrast, we found that since the 1980s—when, not coincidentally, the hearings began to be televised—partisanship has played a much bigger role than nominee candor. Simply put, the threats that we saw from Senators Schumer, Lemieux, and others appear to be empty. Senators do not reject nominees for being too evasive—and because the nominees probably know this, they continue to answer fewer questions than they probably could.

A More Modest Proposal

So where does this leave us? Existing proposals to improve the hearings have fallen short. Yet most commentators, including us, would acknowledge that the hearings could be improved somewhat. Is there any way to make that happen? We think there may be.

First, at a general level, we reiterate that we think our findings about nominee responsiveness—and in particular, the discovery that nominees have always exhibited roughly the same mix of forthcoming responses and not forthcoming responses—should fundamentally shift the terms of the debate about confirmation hearings. Specifically, rather than arguing that the hearings have *become* less substantive, or that things now are worse than they used to be, critics should acknowledge that nominees have not changed all that much in recent years. Thus whatever criticism one wishes to level at the hearing process should be leveled at the *entire* process, not just nominees since the 1980s.

Again, we think this is an important corrective because it forces reformers to examine whether the process has *ever* worked, and whether nominees have *ever* delivered the kind of candid responses that we might want them to. Rather than focusing on Bork's hearing and assuming that his candor taught subsequent nominees to be evasive, critics should ask whether there is something about the process itself that has never been able to generate sufficiently forthcoming or satisfying answers. At a minimum, therefore, we hope that our work here will encourage those interested in improving the hearings to attack the problem at its source, rather than focusing on recent nominee behavior. This should improve the effectiveness of whatever proposals others may develop in the future.

In the meantime, we think that the findings we have offered here can be used to some effect by those who are dissatisfied with the hearing process. Our proposal is as follows. Recall that in chapter 4, nominees on average provide forthcoming answers to roughly 65 percent of the questions they are asked. They give qualified answers to another 25 percent, and decline to answer only about 10 percent. These figures vary by nominee, of course, but they are stable enough to establish a reliable baseline number. Our view is that senators could use this baseline to hold nominees to a standard of responsiveness. For example, if a nominee were to provide forthcoming answers to only 55 percent of their questions, and decline to answer another 20 percent, this should raise a "red flag" for senators concerned with candor. It would also give those senators a powerful piece of objective evidence to justify a "no" vote should they wish to use it. Over the long haul, as senators began to hold nominees to this sort of responsiveness standard, our expectation is that nominees would be—at the very least—unlikely to drop below historic norms in terms of their candor.

More optimistically, we think it is not implausible that with the specter of this baseline hovering above their hearings, nominees might make an effort to stay above—perhaps even well above—this average.

We acknowledge, of course, that this proposal is unlikely to transform the hearings overnight. As we noted earlier, nominees have little incentive under the current arrangement to provide more information than they need to. But we do think that our "responsiveness standard" proposal is a step in the right direction, in large part because it focuses more on senators than on nominees. One of the reasons that we believe senators have been making empty threats about voting "no" on evasive nominees but not following through is that they have lacked an empirically grounded metric like the one we provide here. That is, in the past senators may have had a *sense* that certain nominees were not answering as many questions as they should, but they had no way to back it up. But now they have one that is reliable and accessible. Moreover, it is both easy to understand—it is essentially a score on a 1 to 100 scale—and it works across time, applying to every nominee who has had a hearing since 1955.

Simply put, we think our method could provide senators with a powerful tool for assessing nominees where previously there was none. How they might use it, of course, would vary. Some could insist that no nominee drop below the historic average for previous hearings—roughly 65 percent forthcoming responses, and no more than 10 percent not forthcoming. Others could focus on specific kinds of questions—say, for example, civil liberties issues—and measure nominees that way. Still others might continue to rely on consider- ations outside of nominee responsiveness to make their decisions. But we think that this standard gives those senators who are interested in using it a way to make sure that nominees are, at the very least, remaining consistent with their predecessors.

In truth, however, we are not sure that there is a pressing need to overhaul the hearings. They may be imperfect, but they have been that way from the start. As such, our view is that if anything is in need of change, it is probably the overall perception of the hearings, rather than the hearings themselves. We believe that the stakes of the "vapid and hollow charade" narrative—or what might better be described as a misperception—are actually quite high.

First, from a practical perspective, we think it is entirely possible that sena- tors at some point may actually reject a nominee because they mistakenly believe that he or she was more evasive than his predecessors. As we discussed in chapter 5, we do not have evidence that this has happened yet, but our concern is that it might. Voting against confirmation of a Supreme Court nominee is a serious step. And while it may often be justified, it should at least be based on accurate information. The prospect that any important political decision might be made on false premises is quite troubling.

Our second concern is that if this misperception of nominee evasiveness persists, confidence in the Court might erode, even if only slightly. The confirmation process serves an important role in providing democratic accountability to the Court. This accountability helps the public trust the Court as a legitimate institution. And to the extent that the Court depends on such legitimacy to function effectively (see, e.g., Caldeira and Gibson 1992), it is entirely possible that respect for the Court, or even adherence to its rulings—by lower courts, elected officials, or the people themselves—might begin to wane if there is a real loss in confidence in the hearings and the nominees. (See also Gibson and Caldeira [2009], who found that focus on the "politics" of the confirmation process can reduce the legitimacy of the Court.)

Clearly, then, the widespread misunderstanding about evasiveness in Supreme Court confirmation hearings has potentially problematic consequences. Our hope is that the findings we have presented here should help restore at least a bit of confidence in the process.

Notes

CHAPTER ONE

1. As we discuss at length in chapter 2, before 1868, nominations went to committee or to the full Senate without hearings. Between 1868 and 1929, three nominees had very limited hearings. Between 1929 and 1954, nominees had hearings but did not often appear or give testimony.

2. As we discuss in chapter 2, Southern senators on the Judiciary Committee saw Justice Harlan's 1954 confirmation hearing as an opportunity to stall the implementation of the Court's ruling in *Brown*.

CHAPTER TWO

1. Specter is quoted in Kagan 2010, 63.

2. Though in later years, advice has come to mean the president consulting with senators on potential nominees.

3. Much of the history in this section comes from an invaluable *Congressional Research Service* report by Rutkus and Bearden (2009), and from the excellent historical sections in Ringhand and Collins (2011).

4. Most historians acknowledge that Brandeis's hearings were "laced with anti-Semitism" and efforts to prevent Brandeis from becoming the Court's first Jewish justice (Wittes 2009, 45).

5. Rutkus and Bearden report that between 1923 and 1946 most nominees were actually referred to a subcommittee first, and then to the full Judiciary Committee (7).

6. This applies, of course, only to nominees who advanced to the hearing stage, not those who were withdrawn before they got to a hearing, such as Douglas Ginsburg and Harriet Miers.

7. Even Carswell's defenders in the Senate were lukewarm in their support, often attempting to recast his "mediocrity" as an asset rather than a liability. For example, Louisiana senator Russell Long said, "Does it not seem that we have had enough of those upside down, corkscrew thinkers? Would it not appear that it might be well to take a B student or a C student who was able to think straight, compared to one of those A students who are capable of the kind of thinking that winds up getting a 100% increase in crime in this country?" Senator Roman Hruska added, "There are a lot of mediocre judges and people and lawyers, they are entitled to a little representation, aren't they? We can't have all Brandeises, Frankfurters, and Cardozos" (*Time* 1970).

8. The House started televising regular business on C-SPAN in April of 1979, but the full Senate did not even consider a resolution to allow coverage of the Senate floor's regular business until 1984. It was defeated at first, but in July 1986 the Senate allowed coverage on a permanent basis (Crain and Goff 1988).

9. Our method for identifying and counting questions is discussed in detail in the next chapter. See also Ringhand and Collins (2011) for similar findings.

10. Figure 2.2 graphs the number of senators that had exchanges with each nominee, with black bars representing senators that had exchanges and gray bars representing senators that did not have exchanges. The overall size of the bars combined represents the total number of senators on the Judiciary Committee.

11. The outliers here are the same as in figure 2.1: Marshall, Haynsworth, Bork, and Thomas. For reasons explained earlier, these four hearings were unusually long, resulting in a higher per-senator average than the overall trend would indicate.

12. The Bricker Amendments were proposed constitutional amendments to limit the treaty power of the U.S. government and the president's ability to enter into executive agreements with foreign powers.

13. In fact, it may have started before Harlan as well. Years earlier, Felix Frankfurter expressed strong reservations about answering specific questions, arguing instead that his confirmation should turn on his past record, not his current views—a strategy that Ruth Bader Ginsburg would years later call the "Frankfurter tradition" (Ginsburg 1988). Moreover, as we noted earlier, some nominees between Frankfurter in 1939 and Harlan in 1955 were disinclined to accept the Committee's invitation to testify at all. Thus even before Harlan there was a certain degree of hesitancy on the part of prospective justices when it came to answering questions at their hearings.

14. Somewhat infamously, Scalia (33) took this policy so seriously that he even refused to give a firm answer to his views on *Marbury v. Madison*.

15. Of course, the question of whether recent nominees engage in these kinds of maneuvers *more* than their predecessors is a critically important one, and we address it in depth in subsequent chapters.

16. We relied exclusively on the *New York Times* because it was one of the few papers whose coverage spans the entire period, providing us with the longitudinal perspective that we needed.

CHAPTER THREE

1. All hearing transcripts since 1971 are available online at the U.S. Senate's website (see http://www.gpo.gov/fdsys/browse/committee.action?chamber=senate &committee=judiciary). Transcripts prior to that time are on microfiche or hardbound copy.

2. We discuss intercoder reliability later in the chapter.

3. In our prior published work based on this project, we used the terms "candid" and "candor" to describe what we now call "forthcoming" or "responsive." In those previous efforts, "candor" was not used to imply anything about the honesty of the response, but rather the degree to which the responses were forthcoming.

4. Farganis was the principal coder, analyzing all of the transcripts. The second coder was a graduate student. Wedeking was responsible for calculating the reliability scores.

CHAPTER FOUR

1. Herbert 2006, A15.

2. Given that Kennedy's hearings came about as a result of Bork's failed confirmation, it is certainly surprising—if not ironic as well—that Kennedy was slightly more responsive than Bork even though it is widely believed that Bork's candor was what doomed him.

3. A detailed explanation of each of these coding categories, as well as examples, can be found in chapter 3.

4. To reiterate a point from chapter 3, we use the term "evasiveness" simply to mean not answering in a Forthcoming manner. Unless explicitly stated, we do not attach any particular motive to the nominee's "evasiveness."

5. When we created a similarly styled figure based on Less-Than-Forthcoming answers, we see a similar image.

6. The largest QOF category is composed of miscellaneous and other topics that did not lend themselves to easy classification. However, we note that a large bulk of QOFs focused on legal education, experience, and training (27.1%).

7. We use a standard ideological distance measure, estimated from ideal points for members of Congress and nominees. We used Common Space Scores (Poole 1998) for members of Congress, and then transformed them to the same "space" as nominees, following Epstein, Segal, and Westerland (2008), and then took the absolute squared difference.

8. The other two potential units of analysis seem less appropriate for what we are trying to learn about confirmation hearings in this chapter. Examining responsiveness at the "question level" would be beneficial if we wanted to determine what factors influenced any given response, but less helpful for understanding how responses vary across senators and time. The other option, examining responsiveness at the "nominee level" would be beneficial if we wanted to determine system level factors, but would be silent on factors that vary from senator to senator, or within particular nominees. Additionally, we would be greatly constrained with only 30 observations.

9. For the percentage of questions focusing on a nominee's views, and the percentage of questions focusing on civil liberties issues, we gathered this data ourselves according to the guidelines outlined above. For the ideology variable, see our explanation earlier in this chapter. For partisanship, we used the "bioguide" of Congress, found online at http://bioguide.congress.gov/biosearch/biosearch.asp.

10. Thornberry is excluded here because he did not receive a vote.

11. We also tried the natural log of the number of questions and the results are nearly identical.

12. Our source for the measurement of divided government was obtained from http://www.senate.gov/pagelayout/history/one_item_and_teasers/partydiv.htm and http://history.house.gov/Institution/Party-Divisions/Party-Divisions/.

13. Our source for this variable is Segal and Cover (1989), with data updated by Segal at http://www.stonybrook.edu/polsci/jsegal/qualtable.pdf.

CHAPTER FIVE

1. Scalia is something of an outlier in this post-O'Connor period. This may have been because he was such a universally respected nominee, and because the norm of universal question-asking had not quite set in by that time. An additional possibility is that Scalia's confirmation hearing is somewhat unique for this era in the sense that it occurred directly on the heels of Rehnquist's Chief Justice hearing.

2. A box and whisker plot provides crucial information about how "all" of the committee members treated the nominee relative to one another, not just as an "average." Specifically, the "box" portion represents 50% of the senators, with the top, horizontal line of the box representing the 25th percentile and the bottom horizontal line of the box representing the 75th percentile. The horizontal line in the middle of the box represents the mean (or average). That is to say, the middle horizontal line will correspond with the means depicted in figure 2.3. The whiskers represent the remaining portions of the data, with the top whisker corresponding to the 1st–25th percentile, while the bottom whisker corresponds to the bottom 25% of the data. Importantly, any "dots" in figure 5.2 represent outliers that suggest that

nominee received an especially high number of questions from a senator compared to the rest of the senators.

3. Perhaps even more remarkable is the fact that Marshall gave forthcoming answers 76% of the time.

4. Two notes should be made about the data in Garrett and Rutkus (2010). First, because of the recent nature of Kagan's hearings, there were no dates for her. Thus, we manually calculated the number of days based on the appropriate dates to fill in the missing blank. Second, the number of days for John Roberts in figure 5.3 is substantially larger than that listed in Garrett and Rutkus (2010) and is also based on a manual calculation. This is because Roberts's unique circumstances when the president withdrew the nomination to renominate Roberts for the Chief Justice position. Thus, we believe it is more appropriate to count the days the Senate *first* started to prepare for John Roberts, when he was initially nominated as an associate justice, not from when he was nominated as Chief Justice. In other words, we combine the two time periods.

5. The only nominee during the pretelevision era that shows any resemblance to the television era is Stewart, but he was a recess appointment whose hearing was held months after he was already seated on the Court.

6. We acknowledge that one could also examine the number of days from the time a vacancy occurs to the first hearing because the Senate's preparation may contribute to the delay during this time. Indeed, as scholars such as Nemacheck (2007) have noted, the Senate's "advice" function means that senators do play some role in suggesting to the president who should be nominated, which in turn means that the Senate can be at least partly responsible for explaining the number of days between a vacancy and when the nominee is announced. However, as Nemacheck (2007) notes, while presidents have allowed senators to have a voice in the selection process, this has not been consistent across or within presidential administrations. We prefer, therefore, to count the number of days from the date of the nominee announcement to the first hearing because that time period is largely controlled by the Senate, whereas the earlier time period is largely controlled by the president.

7. Interestingly, this parallels research by Hetherington (2001) who found that elite polarization in Congress (around the same time) led to an increase in party importance and salience of the parties for citizens.

8. We note that while several studies examine the final floor vote (e.g., Cameron, Cover, and Segal 1990; Epstein et al. 2006), we know of no other study that analyzes the committee votes of Senate Judiciary Committee members.

9. Two examples illustrate this point. For Clarence Thomas, the new motion was to send the nomination to the floor without recommendation, while for Robert Bork it was to send the nomination to the floor with an unfavorable recommenda-

tion. In the analyses below, we focus only on Bork's and Thomas's first committee vote.

10. Senate data available at http://www.judiciary.senate.gov/nominations/ SupremeCourt/CommitteeVotes.cfm.

11. This is supported by a quote from Senator Lindsey Graham's opening statement at Sonia Sotomayor's hearing: "Unless you have a complete meltdown, you are going to get confirmed. . . . I do not think you will [have a meltdown]."

12. There were a total of 473 senator- vote opportunities for the 29 confirmation hearings, which excludes Thornberry because he did not have a Committee vote. However, two senators voted "present" and eight more senators were absent, reducing the total to 463 votes cast, of which 384 were yes votes (82.9%).

13. It is important to remember that most senators, prior to the questioning at the confirmation hearings, have already met privately with the nominee and may have received some additional information during those meetings (Rutkus 2005). Moreover, many senators have already met privately with the president during the selection phase. Unfortunately, there is no way to track the occurrences of these meetings for all nominees over time or even to try to account for what was said in the private meetings. If anything, it contributes to our expectation that nominee responsiveness should not have an influence on senators' votes during the televised hearings.

14. It is important to note that our analysis includes 122 senators' votes even though they did not ask any questions. We included them here to avoid "throwing away" data. Because it was fairly common for senators to not ask questions during the early confirmation hearings, these 122 senators did not have a responsiveness "score." This creates a dilemma: How will our analysis treat those 122 observations? We saw three options: (1) exclude them; (2) substitute or impute the mean level of responsiveness for each nominee; or (3) run a selection model to account for possible "selection bias" (i.e., to account for the possibility that senators who do not ask questions are more likely to vote "yes"). We tried these three different strategies and all of which returned the same result. Therefore, we resolved this dilemma by imputing the mean level of responsiveness for each nominee for each missing senator. This seems justified based on the argument that if a senator did not ask any questions, but listened to the hearings, he or she would come away with the "average" sense of responsiveness for the nominee. As an alternative modeling strategy, and to ensure the robustness of our approach, we also estimated the same model but excluded the 122 senators who did not ask a question. The results are nearly identical (see also Wedeking and Farganis 2010). Lastly, we also checked another alternative to see whether there were any "selection bias" problems with those senators who did not ask any questions yet still voted. Specifically, it might be problematic to include them in the analysis (with the imputed mean value of responsive-

ness) and, at the same time, it might be problematic to exclude them altogether. Thus, we estimated a Heckman sample selection probit model. This process entails estimating two equations and tests whether the two processes are related. The two processes are (1) whether a senator asks a question (yes or no); and (2) whether the senator voted favorably (yes or no)? Importantly, in the second model we included the appropriate interaction variables that we use in this chapter and the results are the same. Moreover, the rho coefficient of the Heckman model, which tests for the correlation or relationship between the two stages (the selection stage of "asking a question" and the outcome stage of "favorable vote or not") and it was *not* significant. This indicates that there is no relationship between whether a senator asks a question and how they voted on the nominee. In summary, regardless of our measurement and modeling choices, we get the same results.

15. We obtained each senator's partisanship from http://bioguide.congress.gov/biosearch/biosearch.asp.

16. http://www.senate.gov/pagelayout/history/one_item_and_teasers/party-div.htm and http://history.house.gov/Institution/Party-Divisions/Party-Divisions/.

17. We should also note that there is no correlation between a nominee's degree of forthcomingness and the number of "yes" votes by the full Senate on the final confirmation vote.

CHAPTER SIX

1. Precise figures indicating the size of the audience for most of the hearings are not available in large part because C-SPAN does not participate in Nielsen ratings.

2. We did not include "Index" or "News Summary" articles, or articles that briefly mentioned that a nominee was attending some event. We did include articles that referred to opinions of the president or senators when referencing the nomination, and also letters to the editor.

3. To be perfectly clear, we are not suggesting that recent nominees are consistently *worse* at answering questions than their predecessors; as we have demonstrated throughout this book, they are not. But because critics tend to romanticize the earlier hearings—the point we made in the previous section—when recent nominees do not answer every question in a completely satisfying manner, it helps fuel the perception that the hearings have become less substantive.

4. Some of the example excerpts have been edited for space considerations. Any removed text is noted by an ellipsis.

5. ABA Model Code of Judicial Conduct, Canon 2, Rule 2.11(A)(5) (2007). But some commentators disagree with the claim that the ABA Canon shields nominees from answering any questions about their judicial philosophy (Goldberg 2004).

6. To better understand the meaning of the memo, it is important to have some background information. Prior to this, Sandra Day O'Connor had sent a letter to Senator Jesse Helms discussing her beliefs about the proper role of questioning and her reluctance to say too much about future cases. The key issue at the heart of the matter stemmed from an argument made by Grover Rees, a law professor, who argued that nominees could talk candidly about how they might decide future cases as long as everyone understood that no promises were made, and Rees justified this argument on the grounds there was some precedent established along these lines by previous nominees in earlier hearings.

Regarding the Rees memo, John Roberts responded to O'Connor with reassurances that her view need not be modified. Specifically, with respect to the separation of powers concerns, Roberts argued that the views of law professor Grover Rees were incorrect. Specifically, Rees's arguments were, as paraphrased by Roberts, that nominees could answer questions about "actual (though nonpending) or hypothetical cases" and that if a nominee stated her views, it would *not* be grounds for disqualifying oneself from deciding the case. Recall, the apparent "loophole" provided for by Rees's argument was that there was a mutual understanding that "no promises" were made. Rees later went on to publish his arguments (Rees 1982–83).

7. Source of memo: http://www.archives.gov/news/john-roberts/accession-60-88-0498/026-oconnor-misc/folder026.pdf.

8. Though we should also note that the small variations in question wording, given the consistency in table 6.1, reassure us that these results are robust despite small, minor changes in question focus (e.g., the question is on abortion as opposed to all issues).

9. Although we searched for surveys about other nominees, we were unable to find any others with questions that were sufficiently similar for comparative purposes.

10. In fact, some questions for Roberts and Kagan are split-sample questions. For example, half of the respondents were asked about Kagan answering questions about "past cases" while the other half of the respondents were asked about "her position on abortion." The fact that the focus of the question shifts slightly while the results are very similar suggests that the public has a strong appetite for knowing more about the nominees if they only consider this in a simple manner, regardless of the singular focus.

CHAPTER SEVEN

1. This connection was even more tenuous prior to the 1913 ratification of the Seventeenth Amendment, which allowed for direct election of senators. Until that time, senators were elected by state legislatures, which were directly elected by voters in the state.

References

ABC News/Washington Post Clarence Thomas Hearing Poll. 1991. September. (ICPSR 9767, Question #22).

ABC News/Washington Post Supreme Court Poll. 2005. July. (ICPSR Study #4332).

Alito, Samuel A. 2006. *Senate Committee on the Judiciary: S. Hrg. 109–277, Confirmation Hearing on the Nomination of Samuel A. Alito, Jr. to be an Associate Justice of the Supreme Court of the United States.* Washington, DC: Government Printing Office.

Althaus, Scott L., and Young Mie Kim. 2006. "Priming Effects in Complex Environments." *Journal of Politics* 68 (November): 960–76.

American Bar Association Model Code of Judicial Conduct. http://www.american bar.org/groups/professional_responsibility/publications/model_code_of_judi cial_conduct.html.

Anderson, Craig A., Mark R. Lepper, and Lee Ross. 1980. "Perseverance of Social Theories: The Role of Explanation in the Persistence of Discredited Information." *Journal of Personality and Social Psychology* 39 (6): 1037–49.

Baumgartner, Frank R., Suzanna L. De Boef, and Amber E. Boydstun. 2008. *The Decline of the Death Penalty and the Discovery of Innocence.* Cambridge: Cambridge University Press.

Baumgartner, Frank R., and Bryan D. Jones. 2009. *Agendas and Instability in American Politics.* 2nd ed. Chicago: University of Chicago Press.

Bell, Lauren Cohen. 2002. *Warring Factions: Interest Groups, Money, and the New Politics of Senate Confirmation.* Columbus: Ohio State University Press.

Benson, Robert W. 2010. "The Senate Farce for Kagan's Confirmation to the Supreme Court." *Huffington Post.* June 7. http://huff.to/cV2I34.

Berke, Richard L. 1991. "Panel Plans to Press Court Nominee." *New York Times*, July 3, D18.

Blackmun, Harry A. 1970. *Hearing on the Nomination of Harry A. Blackmun to be Associate Justice of the Supreme Court.* Washington, DC: Government Printing Office.

Bork, Robert H. 1987. *Nomination of Robert H. Bork to Be Associate Justice of the Supreme Court of the U.S.* Washington, DC: Government Printing Office.

Bork, Robert H. 1990. *The Tempting of America: The Political Seduction of the Law.* New York: Free Press.

Brambor, Thomas, William Roberts Clark, and Matt Golder. 2006. "Understanding Interaction Models: Improving Empirical Analyses." *Political Analysis* 14:63–82.

Brennan, William. 1957. *Hearings before the Committee on the Judiciary, U.S. Senate, on the Nomination of William J. Brennan, Jr., to be an Associate Justice of the U.S. Supreme Court, 85th Cong.,1st Sess.* Washington, DC: Government Printing Office.

Breyer, Stephen G. 1994. *Senate Committee on the Judiciary: S. Hrg. 103–715, Hearings on the Nomination of Stephen G. Breyer to be an Associate Justice of the Supreme Court of the United States.* Washington, DC: Government Printing Office.

Burger, Warren. 1969. *Hearing on Nomination of Warren E. Burger to be Chief Justice of the United States before the Senate Committee on the Judiciary, 91st Cong., 1st Sess.* Washington, DC: Government Printing Office.

Cable News Ratings. 2009. "Cable News Ratings for Tuesday, July 14, 2009." http://tvbythenumbers.zap2it.com/2009/07/15/cable-news-ratings-for-tuesday-july-14-2009/22901/.

Caldeira, Gregory A., and James L. Gibson. 1992. "The Etiology of Public Support for the Supreme Court." *American Journal of Political Science* 43 (August): 635–64.

Caldeira, Gregory A., and Charles E. Smith Jr. 1996. "Campaigning for the Supreme Court: The Dynamics of Public Opinion on the Thomas Nomination. *Journal of Politics* 58 (3): 655–81.

Cameron, Charles M., Albert D. Cover, and Jeffrey A. Segal. 1990. "Senate Voting on Supreme Court Nominees: A Neoinstitutional Model." *American Political Science Review* 84 (2): 525–34.

Carmody, John. 1986. "The TV Column." *Washington Post,* August 6, D8.

Carson, Jamie L. 2008. "Electoral Accountability, Party Loyalty, and Roll-Call Voting in the U.S. Senate." In *Why Not Parties? Party Effects in the United States Senate,* edited by Nathan W. Monroe, Jason M. Roberts, and David W. Rohde. Chicago: University of Chicago Press.

Carswell, Harrold George. 1970. *Nomination of George Harrold Carswell to be Asso-*

ciate Justice of the Supreme Court of the United States: Hearings before the Senate Comm. on the Judiciary, 91st Cong., 2d Sess. Washington, DC: Government Printing Office.

Carter, Stephen L. 1988. "Essays on the Supreme Court Appointment Process: The Confirmation Mess." *Harvard Law Review* 101 (April): 1185.

Carter, Stephen L. 1994. *The Confirmation Mess: Cleaning Up the Federal Appointments Process.* New York: Basic Books.

Carter, Stephen L. 2009. "Let the Nominee Stay Home." Op-ed. *New York Times,* May 10, WK9.

Comiskey, Michael. 2004. *Seeking Justices: The Judging of Supreme Court Nominees.* Lawrence: University Press of Kansas.

Cowden, Jonathan A. 2001. "Southernization of the Nation and Nationalization of the South: Racial Conservatism, Social Welfare, and White Partisans in the United States, 1956–92." *British Journal of Political Science* 31 (2): 277–301.

Cox, Gary W., and Mathew D. McCubbins. 1993. *Legislative Leviathan.* Berkeley: University of California Press.

Crain, W. Mark, and Brian L. Goff. 1988. *Televised Legislatures: Political Information Technology and Public Choice.* Boston: Kluwer Academic.

Cross, Frank B. 2007. *Decision Making in the U.S. Courts of Appeals.* Stanford: Stanford University Press.

C-SPAN. 2012. "Cameras in the Court Timeline." http://www.c-span.org/The-Courts/Cameras-in-The-Court-Timeline/.

Czarnezki, Jason J., William K. Ford, and Lori A. Ringhand. 2007. "An Empirical Analysis of the Confirmation Hearings of the Justices of the Rehnquist Natural Court." *Constitutional Commentary* 24:127–98.

Dahl, Robert A. 1957. "Decision-Making in a Democracy: The Supreme Court as a National Policy-Maker." *Journal of Public Law* 6:279–95.

Dancey, Logan, Kjersten R. Nelson, and Eve M. Ringsmuth. 2011. "'Strict Scrutiny?' The Content of Senate Judicial Confirmation Hearings during the George W. Bush Administration." *Judicature* 95 (3): 126–35.

Derby, Kevin. 2010. "Florida Politicians Toe Party Lines on Elena Kagan Confirmation: Newest U.S. Supreme Court Justice Provokes Mixed Commentary." *Sunshine St. News,* August 6, http://www.sunshinestatenews.com/story/florida-politicians-divide-party-lines-over-elena-kagan-confirmation-supreme-court.

"Eisenhower Names U.S. Judge Harlan to Supreme Court." 1954. *New York Times,* November 9, 1.

"Eisenhower Scores Delay on Harlan." 1955. *New York Times,* February 3, 14.

Eisgruber, Christopher L. 2007. *The Next Justice: Repairing the Supreme Court Appointments Process.* Princeton: Princeton University Press.

Epstein, Lee, Valerie Hoekstra, Jeffrey A. Segal, and Harold J. Spaeth. 1998. "Do

Political Preferences Change? A Longitudinal Study of U.S. Supreme Court Justices." *Journal of Politics* 60 (3): 801–18.

Epstein, Lee, Rene Lindstadt, Jeffrey A. Segal, and Chad Westerland. 2006. "The Changing Dynamics of Senate Voting on Supreme Court Nominees." *Journal of Politics* 68 (2): 296–307.

Epstein, Lee, and Jeffrey A. Segal. 2000. "Measuring Issue Salience." *American Journal of Political Science* 44 (1): 66–83.

Epstein, Lee, Jeffrey A. Segal, Harold J. Spaeth, and Thomas G. Walker. 2007. *The Supreme Court Compendium: Data, Decisions, and Developments*. 4th ed. Washington, DC: CQ Press.

Epstein, Lee, Jeffrey A. Segal, Nancy Staudt, and Rene Lindstadt. 2005. "The Role of Qualifications in the Confirmation of Nominees to the U.S. Supreme Court." *Florida State University Law Review* 32 (4): 1145–73.

Epstein, Lee, Jeffrey A. Segal, and Chad Westerland. 2008. "The Increasing Importance of Ideology in the Nomination and Confirmation of Supreme Court Justices." *Drake Law Review* 56:609–35.

Epstein, Lee, Thomas G. Walker, Nancy Staudt, Scott Hendrickson, and Jason Roberts. 2010. "The U.S. Supreme Court Justices Database." January 26. Chicago: Northwestern University School of Law. http://epstein.usc.edu/research/jus ticesdata.html.

Farganis, Dion, and Justin Wedeking. 2011. "'No Hints, No Forecasts, No Previews': An Empirical Analysis of Supreme Court Nominee Candor from Harlan to Kagan." *Law and Society Review* 45 (3): 525–60.

Fein, Bruce. 1989. "Commentary: A Circumscribed Senate Confirmation Role." *Harvard Law Review* 102 (3): 672–87.

Fitzpatrick, Brian. 2009. "Confirmation 'Kabuki' Does No Justice." *Politico*. Web. June 20. http://politi.co/XhNsc.

Fortas, Abe. 1965. *Hearings on Nomination of Abe Fortas to be Associate Justice of the Supreme Court before the Senate Judiciary Committee, 89th Cong., 1st Sess.* Washington, DC: Government Printing Office.

Fortas, Abe. 1968. *Nominations of Abe Fortas, to be Chief Justice of Supreme Court, and Homer Thornberry, to be Associate Justice of Supreme Court, 90th Cong., 2nd Sess.* Washington, DC: Government Printing Office.

Garrett, R. Sam, and Denis Steven Rutkus. 2010. "Speed of Presidential and Senate Actions on Supreme Court Nominations, 1900–2010." *CRS Report for Congress*. April 21. Washington, DC: Library of Congress.

Gerhardt, Michael J. 1992. "Divided Justice: A Commentary on the Nomination and Confirmation of Justice Thomas." *George Washington Law Review* 60:969–96.

Gibson, James L., and Gregory A. Caldeira. 2009. *Citizens, Courts, and Confirmations*. Princeton: Princeton University Press.

Gibson, James L., Gregory A. Caldeira, and Lester Kenyatta Spence. 2003. "The Supreme Court and the U.S. Presidential Election of 2000." *British Journal of Political Science* 33:535–56.

Ginsburg, Ruth Bader. 1988. "Confirming Supreme Court Justices: Thoughts on the Second Opinion Rendered by the Senate." *University of Illinois Law Review* 1988 (1): 101–18.

Ginsburg, Ruth Bader. 1993. *Senate Committee on the Judiciary: S. Hrg. 103–482, Nomination of Ruth Bader Ginsburg to be Associate Justice of the Supreme Court of the United States.* Washington, DC: Government Printing Office.

Goldberg, Arthur. 1962. *Hearings on the Nomination of Arthur J. Goldberg to be Associate Justice of the Supreme Court. 87th Cong., 2nd Sess.* Washington, DC: Government Printing Office.

Goldberg, Steven H. 2004. "Putting the Supreme Court Back in Place: Ideology Yes; Agenda No." *Georgetown Journal of Legal Ethics* 17:175–201.

Graham, Fred P. 1967a. "Senate Confirmation of Marshall Delayed by McClellan Questions." *New York Times,* July 14.

Graham, Fred P. 1967b. "Marshall Is Questioned on Fine Points of the Law: Thurmond Presses Nominee to Court with More than 60 Complicated Queries." *New York Times,* July 20.

Graham, Fred P. 1967c. "The Law: Marshall on the Stand." *New York Times,* July 20.

Graham, Fred P. 1968. "Thurmond Prods Fortas to Reply." *New York Times,* July 19.

Graham, Fred P. 1971. "Senate Panel Ends Its Questioning of Powell with No Apparent Opposition to His Court Nomination." *New York Times,* November 9.

Greenbaum, Mark. 2010. "Let's Get Rid of Supreme Court Confirmation Hearings." http://www.salon.com/2010/07/04/kagan_hearings_pointless/.

Greenhouse, Linda. 1981. "O'Connor Hearings Open on a Note of Friendship." *New York Times,* September 10, A1.

Greenhouse, Linda. 1987. "Judge Kennedy Says Rights Are Not Always Spelled Out." *New York Times,* December 15, B16.

Greenhouse, Linda. 1990. "Filling in the Blanks: Judge Seems to Put Big Issues to Rest." *New York Times,* September 15.

Greenhouse, Linda. 1994. "Breyer Has Opportunity to Recount His Story." *New York Times,* July 13.

Guliuzza, Frank, Daniel J. Reagan, and David M. Barrett. 1994. "The Senate Judiciary Committee and Supreme Court Nominees: Measuring the Dynamics of Confirmation Criteria." *Journal of Politics* 56 (3): 773–87.

Harlan, John M. 1955. *Hearings on the Nomination of John Marshall Harlan to be Associate Justice of the Supreme Court. 84th Cong., 1st Sess.* Washington, DC: Government Printing Office.

Hartog, Chris Den, and Nathan W. Monroe. 2011. *Agenda Setting in the U.S. Sen-*

ate: Costly Consideration and Majority Party Advantage. New York: Cambridge University Press.

Haynsworth, Clement F. 1969. *Hearings on the Nomination of Clement F. Haynsworth, Jr. to be Associate Justice of the Supreme Court. 91st Cong., 1st Sess.* Washington, DC: Government Printing Office.

"Haynsworth to Keep Post; Nixon Attacks His Critics." 1969. *New York Times,* July 15, 1.

"The Hearings on Television." 1993. *New York Times,* July 20, A15.

Herbert, Bob. 2006. "Judicial Gag Rule." *New York Times,* January 16, A15.

Hetherington, Marc J. 2001. "Resurgent Mass Partisanship: The Role of Elite Polarization." *American Political Science Review* 95 (3): 619–31.

Hill, Michael. 1991. "An Excruciating Personal Drama Played Out on TV." *Baltimore Sun,* October 16. http://articles.baltimoresun.com/1991-10-16/news/1991289132_1_clarence-thomas-senate-debate-nielsen.

Huston, Luther A. 1955a. "Harlan Hearing Held By Senators: Confirmation Urged by Seven—Methfessel, Renewing Old Feud, Opposed It." *New York Times,* February 25.

Huston, Luther A. 1955b. "Harlan Disavows 'One World' Aims in Senate Inquiry: Nominee for Supreme Court, However, Refuses to Give Forecast of Decisions." *New York Times,* February 26.

Huston, Luther A. 1957. "Brennan Favors Inquiries on Reds: McCarthy Questions Justice on Speeches as Hearing on Nomination Starts." *New York Times,* February 27.

Johnson, Timothy R., Ryan C. Black, Jerry Goldman, and Sarah A. Treul. 2009. "Inquiring Minds Want to Know: Do Justices Tip Their Hands with Questions at Oral Argument in the U.S. Supreme Court?" *Washington University Journal of Law & Policy* 29 (1): 241–61.

Johnson, Timothy R., and Jason Roberts. 2004. "Presidential Capital and the Supreme Court Confirmation Process." *Journal of Politics* 66 (3): 663–83.

"Justices Not Candidates." 1968. Editorial. *New York Times,* September 3, 42.

Kagan, Elena. 1995. "Review: Confirmation Messes, Old and New." Review of *The Confirmation Mess* by Stephen L. Carter. *University of Chicago Law Review* 62 (2): 919–42.

Kagan, Elena. 2010. *Senate Committee on the Judiciary: S. Hrg. 111-1044, The Nomination of Elena Kagan to be an Associate Justice of the Supreme Court of the United States.* Washington, DC: Government Printing Office.

Kamisar, Yale. 1986. "The Rehnquist Court Still Seems an Appointment Away." *New York Times,* September 21, E8.

Kastellec, Jonathan P., Jeffrey R. Lax, and Justin H. Phillips. 2010. "Public Opinion and Senate Confirmation of Supreme Court Nominees." *Journal of Politics* 72 (3): 767–84.

Kennedy, Anthony M. 1987. *Senate Committee on the Judiciary: S. Hrg. 100–1037, Nomination of Anthony M. Kennedy to be Associate Justice of the Supreme Court of the United States.* Washington, DC: Government Printing Office.

Krehbiel, Keith. 1991. *Information and Legislative Organization.* Ann Arbor: University of Michigan Press.

Krutz, Glen S., Richard Fleisher, and Jon R. Bond. 1998. "From Abe Fortas to Zoe Baird: Why Some Presidential Nominations Fail in the Senate." *American Political Science Review* 92 (4): 871–81.

Kunda, Ziva. 1990. "The Case for Motivated Reasoning." *Psychological Bulletin* 108 (3): 480–98.

Kyl, Jon. 2010. "Kyl Will Oppose Kagan Nomination." Press Release, Jon Kyl, United States Senator for Arizona, July 20. http://kyl.senate.gov/record.cfm?id=326505.

Leahy, Patrick. 2006. "The Alito Nomination, the Supreme Court, and Presidential Power." Speech delivered at Georgetown Law Center, January 19. http://www.law.georgetown.edu/news/documents/Leahyspeech.pdf.

Lewis, Anthony. 1959. "Stewart Hearing Opens in a Clash: Senators Wrangle over Right to Question on Integration Ruling." *New York Times,* April 10.

Lewis, Neil A. 1990. "Souter Deflects Senators' Queries on Abortion Views: Direct Reply Ruled Out." *New York Times,* September 14, A1.

Lewis, Neil A. 1991. "Frustrated Thomas Panel Ends Hearings with Talk of Overhaul." *New York Times,* September 21, 7.

Lively, Donald E. 1986. "The Supreme Court Appointment Process: In Search of Constitutional Roles and Responsibilities." *Southern California Law Review* 59:551–79.

Long, J. Scott, and Jeremy Freese. 2006. *Regression Models for Categorical Dependent Variables Using Stata.* 2nd ed. College Station, TX: Stata Press.

Maltese, John Anthony. 1995. *The Selling of Supreme Court Nominees.* Baltimore: Johns Hopkins University Press.

Marcus, Ruth. 2010. "Broken Confirmation: High Court Nomination Process Gets Worse." *Washington Post,* online edition, August 11, Opinions. http://www.washingtonpost.com/wpdyn/content/article/2010/08/10/AR2010081004587.html.

Marshall, Thomas R. 1989. "Policymaking and the Modern Court: When Do Supreme Court Rulings Prevail?" *Political Research Quarterly* 42:493–507.

Marshall, Thurgood. 1967. *Nomination of Thurgood Marshall before the Senate Committee on the Judiciary, 90th Congress.* Washington, DC: Government Printing Office.

Martinek, Wendy L., Mark Kemper, and Steven R. Van Winkle. 2002. "To Advise and Consent: The Senate and Lower Federal Court Nominations, 1977–1998." *Journal of Politics* 64 (2): 337–61.

Mayhew, David R. 1974. *Congress: The Electoral Connection.* New Haven: Yale University Press.

McConnell, A. Mitchell, Jr. 1971. "Haynsworth and Carswell: A New Senate Standard of Excellence." *Kentucky Law Journal* 59:42–70.

Molotsky, Irvin, and Warren Weaver Jr. 1986. "Pre-empting Big Bird." *New York Times,* December 10.

Monroe, Nathan W., Jason M. Roberts, and David W. Rohde. 2008. *Why Not Parties? Party Effects in the United States Senate.* Chicago: University of Chicago Press.

Nemacheck, Christine L. 2007. *Strategic Selection: Presidential Nomination of Supreme Court Justices from Herbert Hoover through George W. Bush.* Charlottesville: University of Virginia Press.

O'Brien, David M. 1988. *Judicial Roulette: Report of the Twentieth Century Fund Task Force on Judicial Selection.* New York: Priority Press.

O'Brien, David M. 2011. *Storm Center: The Supreme Court in American Politics, 9th Ed.* New York: W. W. Norton.

O'Connor, Sandra Day. 1981. *Senate Committee on the Judiciary: The Nomination of Judge Sandra Day O'Connor of Arizona to Serve as an Associate Justice of the Supreme Court of the United States.* Washington, DC: Government Printing Office.

"O'Connor to Be First 'Horizon' Guest in New Studio." 2010. January 4. http://www.law.asu.edu/News/CollegeofLawNews.aspx?NewsId=2673.

Overby, L. Marvin, and Robert D. Brown. 1997. "Reelection Constituencies and the Politics of Supreme Court Confirmation Votes." *American Politics Research* 25 (2): 168–78.

Overby, L. Marvin, Beth M. Henschen, Julie Strauss, and Michael H. Walsh. 1994. "African-American Constituents and Supreme Court Nominees: An Examination of the Senate Confirmation of Thurgood Marshall." *Political Research Quarterly* 47 (4): 839–55.

Overby, L. Marvin, Beth M. Henschen, Michael H. Walsh, and Julie Strauss. 1992. "Courting Constituents? An Analysis of the Senate Confirmation Vote on Justice Clarence Thomas." *American Political Science Review* 86 (4): 997–1003.

Palmer, Harvey D., and Justin Wedeking. 2011. "Accounting for Temporal Trends in Party Affect: Negativity versus Neutrality." *Journal of Elections, Public Opinion, and Parties* 21 (1): 57–82.

Poole, Keith T. 1998. "Recovering a Basic Space from a Set of Issue Scales." *American Journal of Political Science* 42 (3): 954–93.

Poole, Keith T., and Howard Rosenthal. 1984. "The Polarization of American Politics." *Journal of Politics* 46 (4): 1061–79.

Post, Robert, and Reva Siegel. 2006. "Questioning Justice: Law and Politics in Judicial Confirmation Hearings." *Yale Law Journal (The Pocket Part)* 115 (January): 38–51.

Powell, Lewis F. 1971. *Senate Committee on the Judiciary: Hearings on the Nominations of William H. Rehnquist, of Arizona, and Lewis F. Powell, Jr. of Virginia, to be Associate Justices of the Supreme Court of the United States.* Washington, DC: Government Printing Office.

Rees, Grover, III. 1982–83. "Questions for Supreme Court Nominees at Confirmation Hearings: Excluding the Constitution." *Georgia Law Review* 17:913–67.

Rehnquist, William H. 1971. *Senate Committee on the Judiciary: Hearings on the Nominations of William H. Rehnquist, of Arizona, and Lewis F. Powell, Jr. of Virginia, to be Associate Justices of the Supreme Court of the United States.* Washington, DC: Government Printing Office.

Rehnquist, William H. 1986. *Senate Committee on the Judiciary: S. Hrg. 99–1067, Nomination of Justice William Hubbs Rehnquist to be Chief Justice of the United States.* Washington, DC: Government Printing Office.

Richards, Mark J., and Herbert M. Kritzer. 2002. "Jurisprudential Regimes in Supreme Court Decision Making." *American Political Science Review* 96:305–20.

Ringhand, Lori A. 2008. "'I'm Sorry, I Can't Answer That': Positive Scholarship and the Supreme Court Confirmation Process." *Journal of Constitutional Law* 10:2–29.

Ringhand, Lori A. 2009. "In Defense of Ideology: A Principled Approach to the Supreme Court Confirmation Process." *William & Mary Bill of Rights Journal* 18: 131–71.

Ringhand, Lori A., and Paul M. Collins. 2011. "May It Please the Senate: An Empirical Analysis of the Senate Judiciary Committee Hearings of Supreme Court Nominees, 1939–2009." *American University Law Review* 60:589–641.

Roberts, John G., Jr. 1981. "Rees Memorandum." Memo written by John Roberts as special assistant to the attorney general sent to Sandra Day O'Connor. http://www.archives.gov/news/john-roberts/accession-60-88-0498/026-oconnor-misc/folder026.pdf.

Roberts, John G., Jr. 2005a. "Oral Argument and the Re-emergence of a Supreme Court Bar." *Journal of Supreme Court History* 30:68–81.

Roberts, John G., Jr. 2005b. *Senate Committee on the Judiciary: S. Hrg. 109–158, Confirmation Hearing on the Nomination of John G. Roberts, Jr. to be Chief Justice of the United States.* Washington, DC: Government Printing Office.

Rotunda, Ronald D. 1995. "Innovations Disguised as Traditions: A Historical

Review of the Supreme Court Nominations Process." *University of Illinois Law Review* 1995 (1): 123–31.

Rotunda, Ronald D. 2001. "The Role of Ideology in Confirming Federal Court Judges." *Georgetown Journal of Legal Ethics* 15:127–41.

Rutkus, Denis Steven. 2005. "Supreme Court Appointment Process: Roles of the President, Judiciary Committee, and Senate." *CRS Report for Congress.* September 1. Washington, DC: Library of Congress.

Rutkus, Denis Steven, and Maureen Bearden. 2009. "Supreme Court Nominations, 1789–2009: Actions by the Senate, the Judiciary Committee, and the President." *CRS Report for Congress.* August 25. Washington, DC: Library of Congress.

Rutkus, Denis Steven, and Maureen Bearden. 2010. "Supreme Court Nominations, 1789–2010: Actions by the Senate, the Judiciary Committee, and the President." *CRS Report for Congress.* August 23. Washington, DC: Library of Congress.

Savage, Charlie, and Sheryl Gay Stolberg. 2010. "Kagan Follows Precedent by Offering Few Opinions." *New York Times,* June 30, A18.

Scalia, Antonin. 1986. *Senate Committee on the Judiciary: S. Hrg. 99-1064, Nomination of Judge Antonin Scalia to be Associate Justice of the Supreme Court of the United States.* Washington, DC: Government Printing Office.

Scherer, Nancy, Brandon L. Bartels, and Amy Steigerwalt. 2008. "Sounding the Fire Alarm: The Role of Interest Groups in the Lower Federal Court Confirmation Process." *Journal of Politics* 70 (4): 1026–39.

Segal, Jeffrey A. 1987. "Senate Confirmation of Supreme Court Justices: Partisan and Institutional Politics." *Journal of Politics* 49 (4): 998–1015.

Segal, Jeffrey A. 2012. Data on website. http://www.stonybrook.edu/commcms/polisci/jsegal/QualTable.pdf.

Segal, Jeffrey A., and Albert D. Cover. 1989. "Ideological Values and the Votes of U.S. Supreme Court Justices." *American Political Science Review* 83 (2): 557–65.

Segal, Jeffrey A., and Harold J. Spaeth. 1996. "The Influence of Stare Decisis on the Votes of United States Supreme Court Justices." *American Journal of Political Science* 40 (4): 971–1003.

Segal, Jeffrey A., and Harold J. Spaeth. 2002. *The Supreme Court and the Attitudinal Model Revisited.* Cambridge: Cambridge University Press.

Shipan, Charles R. 2008. "Partisanship, Ideology, and Senate Voting on Supreme Court Nominees." *Journal of Empirical Legal Studies* 5 (1): 55–76.

Sniderman, Paul M., and Sean M. Theriault. 2004. "The Dynamics of Political Argument and the Logic of Issue Framing." In *Studies in Public Opinion: Attitudes, Nonattitudes, Measurement Error, and Change,* edited by Willem E. Saris and Paul M. Sniderman. Princeton: Princeton University Press.

Sotomayor, Sonia. 2009. *Senate Committee on the Judiciary: S. Hrg. 111-503, Confirmation Hearing on the Nomination of Hon. Sonia Sotomayor, to be an Associate*

Justice of the Supreme Court of the United States July 13–16, 2009. Washington, DC: Government Printing Office.

Souter, David H. 1990. *Senate Committee on the Judiciary: S. Hrg. 101–1263, Hearings on the Nomination of David H. Souter to be Associate Justice of the Supreme Court of the United States*. Washington, DC: Government Printing Office.

Stern, Seth, and Stephen Wermiel. 2010. *Justice Brennan: Liberal Champion*. Boston: Houghton Mifflin Harcourt.

Stevens, John Paul. 1975. *Senate Committee on the Judiciary: Nomination of John Paul Stevens to be a Justice of the Supreme Court*. Washington, DC: Government Printing Office.

Stewart, Potter. 1959. *Hearings on the Nomination of Potter Stewart to be Associate Justice of the Supreme Court. 86th Cong., 1st Sess.* Washington, DC: Government Printing Office.

Stone, Geoffrey R. 2010. "Understanding Supreme Court Confirmations." *Supreme Court Review* 9:381–467.

Stras, David R., and Ryan W. Scott. 2008. "Review Essay: Navigating the New Politics of Judicial Appointments." *Northwestern University Law Review* 102 (4): 1869–1918.

Strauss, David A., and Cass R. Sunstein. 1992. "The Senate, the Constitution, and the Confirmation Process." *Yale Law Journal* 101 (7): 1491–1524.

Taylor, Stuart. 1986. "Scalia Returns Soft Answers to Senators." *New York Times*, August 6, A1.

"Television Coverage of Senate Hearings." 1994. *New York Times*, July 14, D22.

"Television Coverage of the Hearings." 1991. *New York Times*, September 9, A12.

Thomas, Clarence. 1991. *Senate Committee on the Judiciary: S. Hrg. 102–1084, Hearings on the Nomination of Clarence Thomas to be Associate Justice of the Supreme Court*. In 4 parts. Washington, DC: Government Printing Office.

Thornberry, Homer. 1970. *Nominations of Abe Fortas, to be Chief Justice of Supreme Court, and Homer Thornberry, to be Associate Justice of Supreme Court, 90th Cong., 2nd Sess.* Washington, DC: Government Printing Office.

Thorpe, James A. 1969. "The Appearance of Supreme Court Nominees before the Senate Judiciary Committee." *Journal of Public Law* 18:371–84.

Time Magazine. 1970. "The Supreme Court: A Seat for Mediocrity?" Electronic edition. http://www.time.com/time/magazine/article/0,9171,942208,00.html.

Toner, Robin. 2005. "In Complex Dance, Roberts Pays Tribute to Years of Precedent behind *Roe v. Wade*." *New York Times*, September 14, A24.

Tribe, Lawrence. 1985. *God Save This Honorable Court*. New York: Random House.

Tversky, Amos, and Daniel Kahneman. 1982. "The Framing of Decisions and the Psychology of Choice." In *Question Framing and Response Consistency*, edited by Robin Hogarth. San Francisco: Jossey-Bass.

"TV Programs Today." 1987a. *New York Times,* September 15, A27.

"TV Programs Today." 1987b. *New York Times,* December 15, C31.

"TV Programs Today." 1990. *New York Times,* September 13, A18.

Watson, George, and John Stookey. 1995. *Shaping America: The Politics of Supreme Court Appointments.* New York: HarperCollins College.

Wedeking, Justin, and Dion Farganis. 2010. "The Candor Factor: Does Nominee Evasiveness Affect Judiciary Committee Support for Supreme Court Nominees?" *Hofstra Law Review* 39 (2): 329–68.

White, Byron. 1962. *Hearings on the Nomination of Byron R. White to be Associate Justice of the Supreme Court. 87th Cong., 2nd Sess.* Washington, DC: Government Printing Office.

Whittaker, Charles. 1957. *Hearings on the Nomination of Charles E. Whittaker to be Associate Justice of the Supreme Court. 85th Cong., 1st Sess.* Washington, DC: Government Printing Office.

Williams, Margaret, and Lawrence Baum. 2006. "Supreme Court Nominees before the Senate Judiciary Committee." *Judicature* 90 (2): 73–80.

Wittes, Benjamin. 2009. *Confirmation Wars: Preserving Independent Courts in Angry Times.* Lanham, MD: Rowman and Littlefield.

Yalof, David A. 2008. "Confirmation Obfuscation: Supreme Court Confirmation Politics in a Conservative Era." In *Studies in Law, Politics, and Society,* vol. 44, edited by Austin Sarat, 143–73. London: Elsevier.

Zaller, John R. 1992. *The Nature and Origins of Mass Opinion.* New York: Cambridge University Press.

Index